THE

PAST AND PRESENT

OF

MILL CREEK VALLEY

BEING

A COLLECTION OF HISTORICAL AND
DESCRIPTIVE SKETCHES OF THAT PART OF

HAMILTON COUNTY, OHIO

CONTAINING

FACTS, INCIDENTS, AND ANECDOTES ILLUSTRATING THE TOILS
AND PRIVATIONS, AS WELL AS THE MANNERS AND
CUSTOMS, OF THE EARLY SETTLERS

ALSO,

PEN-PORTRAITS OF THE VILLAGES, SUBURBAN RESIDENCES,
AND OTHER IMPROVEMENTS, DESIGNED TO SHOW THE
GROWTH AND DEVELOPMENT OF THIS VALLEY

Henry B. Teetor

HERITAGE BOOKS
2014

HERITAGE BOOKS

AN IMPRINT OF HERITAGE BOOKS, INC.

Books, CDs, and more—Worldwide

For our listing of thousands of titles see our website
at
www.HeritageBooks.com

A Facsimile Reprint
Published 2014 by
HERITAGE BOOKS, INC.
Publishing Division
5810 Ruatan Street
Berwyn Heights, Md. 20740

Originally published

Cohen & Co., Printers
Cincinnati
1882

International Standard Book Numbers
Paperbound: 978-1-55613-748-8
Clothbound: 978-0-7884-9099-6

THE

PAST AND PRESENT

OF

MILL CREEK VALLEY,

BEING

*A COLLECTION OF HISTORICAL AND DESCRIPTIVE
SKETCHES OF THAT PART OF HAMILTON
COUNTY, OHIO.*

CONTAINING

FACTS, INCIDENTS, AND ANECDOTES ILLUSTRATING THE TOILS AND
PRIVATIONS, AS WELL AS THE MANNERS AND CUSTOMS,
OF THE EARLY SETTLERS.

ALSO,

PEN-PORTRAITS OF THE VILLAGES, SUBURBAN RESIDENCES, AND
OTHER IMPROVEMENTS, DESIGNED TO SHOW THE GROWTH
AND DEVELOPMENT OF THIS VALLEY.

By HENRY B. TEETOR.

WITH ILLUSTRATION.

COHEN & Co., Printers, Cincinnati.
1882.

Facsimile Reprint

Published 1993 By

HERITAGE BOOKS INC.
1540E Pointer Ridge Place
Bowie, Maryland 20716
(301) 390-7709

ISBN 1-55613-748-6

A Complete Catalog Listing Hundreds
of Titles on
History, Genealogy & Americana
Free on Request

PREFACE.

This humble volume is the work of a gleaner and partial observer in a narrow historical field. Should an occasional fact,

> "Until now hid away
> In the past's valley of Avilion,"

touching the hardships endured by the pioneers in laying the foundations for the wonderful growth and development of this valley, be hereby "precipitated into the opaque sediment of history"— then this pleasurable task shall have met with an adequate reward.

In its preparation many authors have been consulted, and from some, liberal quotations made. To them, in general, most grateful acknowledgments are made.

The writer begs leave to express his deep sense
of gratitude to the following persons for valuable
assistance :

ROBERT CLARKE & CO.; JOHN M. NEWTON,
ESQ., Librarian Y. M. M. L. A.; JOHN G. OLDEN,
ESQ., Author of "Historical Collections in Hamilton County;" COL. S. D. MAXWELL, Supt. Chamber
of Commerce; PROF. FLORIAN GIAUQUE; PROF.
SAMUEL W. WILLIAMS; LEWIS J. CIST, ESQ.; D.
J. KENNEY, ESQ., and HON. SAMUEL F. HUNT.

When the war for the Union closed, the writer found a home in this peaceful, beautiful valley, choosing as a companion for life one of the surviving daughters of the HON. JONATHAN CILLEY, a distinguished pioneer, who, at nine years of age, arrived at Cincinnati, in 1803.

To that

" True and honorable wife,"

This book is affectionately inscribed.

ERRATA.

Page 112, read *Sui generis.*

Page 152, the statement that Mr. Hartwell was not married at this time, is a mistake.

Page 156, in line 14 read "effected."

Page 160, in line 10 read "consummated."

Page 167, in last line read "Camellia and Eglantine."

Page 171, in fourth line read "Alba."

Page 176, for last line of quotation read, "Is ne'er met with elsewhere."

Page 182, in second line of middle quotation read "shade" for *stade.*

Page 185, read "Geddes" for *Gettis.*

Page 203, read "Twin Elms" for *Twin Oaks.*

Page 215, substitute the name of "Josh Billings" for *Mark Twain.*

CONTENTS.

HISTORICAL

AND

DESCRIPTIVE SKETCHES

IN

MILL CREEK VALLEY.

CHAPTER I.

THE DISCOVERY.

TO the West of San Salvador, more than three hundred miles, and more than four hundred years ago, lay a boundless, magnificent continent.

Because Columbus was the first adventurous European who saw that island, and planted the Royal Standard of Spain thereon, October 12, 1492, he is accredited, by universal consent, with the discovery of the main land—a land he never saw, and of the true character of which he was ignorant at his death, suppos-

ing his first discovery to be one of the islands
bordering on the eastern shores of vast and
opulent Asia.

The great admiral knew not that that World
was to be his everlasting monument, when,
with a broken heart, " yet with little apparent
suffering, and in the most Christian spirit of
resignation " he died May 20, 1506.

And yet we must not forget that five centuries before his memorable voyage, a hardy
band of Norwegians had wintered in tents by
the Pocasset river ; and at Point Alderton,
or some neighboring spot below Boston Harbor, the gallant Thorwald Erricsson had been
slain by the arrows of the natives—first of
Europeans, so far as history tells us, whose
bones were laid beneath the soil of Massachu-
setts and hallowed with Christian burial; and
from the same source we learn that in the year
following, *Snorro Karlsefne*, a descendant of
Erricsson, was born, being the first white man
born in America.

For a hundred years afterwards there was
no intellectual curiosity outside of priest craft
and the walls of monasteries.   But the awak-
ening soon afterwards occurred, and for two
centuries prior to the coming of Columbus, as
the great forerunner of Christian civilization,

the progress of European society had been great. He came in the fullness of time.

OUR PREDECESSORS.

As it was in ancient Britain, long before the westward wave of Roman civilization overswept the land of Caractacus and Boadicea, so was it in this undiscovered country, centuries before the coming of Columbus—both were peopled kingdoms.

The Romans were met by Queen Boadicea

> "Standing loftily charioted
> Brandishing in her hand a dart, and rolling glances lioness-like
> Mad and maddening all that heard her in her fierce volubility
> Girt by half the tribes of Britain near the colony Camulodune."

When Sir Walter Raleigh, in 1584, landed with his fleet at Wocoken, off the coast of North Carolina, and took formal possession of the United States in the name of Queen Elizabeth, they were shortly afterwards welcomed and entertained by the wife of Granganimeo, father of Wingina, the King, with the refinements of Arcadian hospitality.

The historian says: The people were most gentle, loving, and faithful, void of all guile and treason, and such as lived after the manner of the golden age.

And yet the same historian adds, that " the wars of these guileless men were cruel and bloody ; that domestic dissensions had almost exterminated whole tribes ; that they employed the basest stratagems against their enemies, and that they too invited men to a feast in order that they might be murdered in the hour of confidence."

As in Britain, so was it in America. There were found antiquities, such as tumuli, earthworks, pottery, weapons and ornaments of a departed race. That the Mound Builders, whoever they were, roamed and monarchized over England and this country ages before its alleged discovery, there is no intelligent doubt. Who were they?

Let Elizabeth Stuart Phelps answer :

" Man who dwelt in caves like cubs, who was without intelligible speech or human sympathy, or the decency of any wild beast known to science ; or it may have been the highly developed savage, whose language resembled the hissing of a serpent ; or of him still ascending in the type, who fed upon the quivering flesh of animals, cultivated what is known as tribal marriage, and buried his dead with awful laughter ; or of him whose war phrase, being interpreted, signifies 'Let us go and eat that nation.'"

CHAPTER II.

NORTH-WEST TERRITORY.

UNDER British Dominion, the magnificent realm of Virginia as originally granted by Queen Elizabeth, was curtailed in the formation of colonies, until the territory only embraced that which constituted the State of Virginia at the close of the revolution. But to her, as a State, belonged that vast region stretching indefinitely westward between the Ohio river and the Lakes, and known as the NORTH-WESTERN TERRITORY. In 1784 Virginia ceded this territory to the United States —"and a most munificent act it was," says Daniel Webster in the United States Senate, "I never reflect upon it without a disposition to do honor and justice, and justice would be the highest honor to Virginia for the cession of her North-western Territory. I will say, sir, it is one of her fairest claims to the respect and gratitude of the Country."

In 1787, Congress organized this territory

and gave it a constitution and provisional
officers. It subsequently divided it; the eastern
portion retaining that historical name, and
embraced the region now included in the
States of Michigan and Ohio. The population of Ohio being at that time about 42,000.

The sixth article of that constitution con-
tained the celebrated provision that there
should be neither slavery nor involuntary ser-
vitude therein, except for the punishment of
crimes. In the light of this fact we see how
munificent the act of Virginia—a Slave State
—was.

This provision it was that gave impetus to
emigration. Henceforth this new, and not the
old Dominion; was to be the ocean to the great
rivers and streams of westward emigration.

"Under the inspiring genius of FREE
LABOR," says Mr. Olden, "Came those
brave men and women, known as the pioneer settlers, and braving the dangers of
savage foes and the toils and privations of a
frontier life, planted their homes in the track-
less wilderness."

Major-General Arthur St. Clair was appointed by President Washington, first Governor of this territory.

THE MIAMIES.

When the pioneers came to this valley, they found it the forest home of Indians, bearing the tribal name of *Miamies*, signifying *mother*. Their territory extended from the Scioto to the Wabash, and from the Ohio to Lake Michigan. This was the territory claimed for them by LITTLE TURTLE, in the Greenville Treaty of 1795.

They were here as far back as 1684, how much earlier, it is not known. They left no history, save what is written on the face of the earth, or concealed in its bosom. They were our predecessors; whence came they? Were they the degenerate descendants of the Mound Builders?

Nature's curtain has dropped upon the part played on the world's stage by that departed race. Man may found institutions with boundless capital, guided by the keenest intellectual research to exhume their history, but they can not part its folds or bid it rise. Why should we seek to extort the secret of their life from the bosom of the all-pitiful earth? That we stand to-day in their stead, by reason of race developement, none will deny; that it is at an end, none will assert; that every one sees, now and then.

"A grace of being, finer than himself,
 That beckons and is gone ; "

that every one feels, now and then

"A larger life upon his own impinging,
 With swift glimpse of spacious circles
 Luminous with mind,"

is the testimony of our consciousness

LITTLE TURTLE

Was a distinguished chief and counsellor
of the Miamies. They called him *Mesh-e-
ken-ogh-qua.* He commanded at the defeat
of General Harmar and afterwards of St.
Clair. He had a soul of fire, and he was
the personification of the rude age in which he
lived. We learn from Mansfield's Memories
that Little Turtle visited this valley after the
battle of Fallen Timber, and that he himself
remembered seeing him at the house of his
father, Col. Jared Mansfield, who then occupied
the Ludlow mansion house (in Cumminsville).
He describes him as a "dark man, with swar-
thy complexion, riding a fine horse," dis-
mounting before his father's house, and after
a consultation with him touching boundary
lines between the two nations—riding rapidly

away never to revisit these scenes again.
"The sun of Indian glory set with him, and
the clouds and shadows which for two hundred years had gathered round their destiny
now closed in the starless night of death."

We annex a sketch of him, taken from
Drake's Indian Biography.

It has been generally said, that had the advice of this chief been taken before their disastrous fight with General Wayne, there is little
doubt but that Wayne would have met with as
ill-success as St. Clair. He was not for fighting
General Wayne at Presque Isle, and inclined
rather to peace than fighting him at all. In a
council held the night before the battle, he
argued as follows: "We have beaten the
enemy twice, under separate commanders.
We cannot expect the same good fortune always to attend us. The Americans are now
led by a chief who never sleeps; the night and
the day are alike to him. And during all the
time that he has been marching upon our villages, notwithstanding the watchfulness of our
young men, we have never been able to surprise him. Think well of it. There is something whispers me, it would be prudent to listen
to his offers of peace." For holding this language, he was reproached by another chief

with cowardice, which put an end to all further discourse. Nothing wounds the feelings of a warrior like the reproach of cowardice, but he stifled his resentment, did his duty in the battle, and his issue proved him a truer prophet than his accuser believed.

Little Turtle lived some years after the war, in great esteem among men of high standing. He was alike courageous and humane, possessing great wisdom. "And," says School-craft, "there has been few individuals among aborigines who have done so much to abolish the rites of human sacrifice. The grave of this noted warrior is shown to visitors near Fort Wayne. It is frequently visited by the Indians in that part of the country, by whom his memory is cherished with the greatest respect and veneration."

When the philosopher and famous traveller, Volney, was in America in the winter of 1797, Little Turtle came to Philadelphia; Volney, hearing of his presence, sought immediate acquaintance with the celebrated chief, for highly valuable purposes, which in some measure he effected. He made a vocabulary of his language, which he printed in the appendix to his travels. A copy in manuscript, more extensive than the printed one, is in the library of the Philosophical Society of Pennsylvania.

Having become convinced that all resistance to the whites was vain, be brought his nation to consent to peace, and to adopt agricultural pursuits. And it was with a view of soliciting Congress and the benevolent Society of Friends, for assistance to effect this latter purpose, that he now visited Philadelphia. While here he was inoculated for the small pox, and was afflicted with the gout and rheumatism.

At the time of Mr. Volney's interview with him for information, he took no notice of the conversation while the interpreter was communicating with Mr. Volney, for he did not understand English, but walked about, plucking out his beard and eye-brows. He was dressed now in English clothes. His skin, where not exposed, Mr. Volney says, was as white as his; and on speaking upon the subject, Little Turtle said, "I have seen Spaniards in Louisiana, and found no difference of color between them and me. And why should there be any? In them, as in us, it is the work of the *father of colors*, the *sun* that burns us. You white people compare the color of your face with that of your bodies." Mr. Volney explained to him the notion of many, that his race was descended from the Tartars, and by a map showed him the supposed communication between Asia and America. To this, Little Turtle replied; "*Why should not those Tartars, who resemble us, have come from America? Are there any reasons to the contrary?* Or why should we not both have been in our own country?" It is a fact that the Indians gave themselves a name which is equivalent to our word *indigine*, that is, *one sprung from the soil*, or natural to it.

When Mr. Volney asked Little Turtle what prevented him from living among the whites, and if he were not more comfortable in Philadelphia than upon the banks of the Wabash, he said: "Taking all things together you have the advantage over us; but here I am deaf and dumb. I do not talk your language; I can neither hear, nor make myself heard. When I walk through the streets, I see every person in his shop employed about something; one makes shoes, another hats, a third sells cloth, and every one lives by his labor. I say to myself which of all these things can you do? Not one. I can make a bow or an arrow, catch fish, kill game, and go to war; but none of these is of any use here. To learn what is done here would require a long time. Old age comes on. I should be a piece of furniture useless to my nation, useless to the

whites, and useless to myself. I must return to my own country."

Col. John Johnston has given in his " Recollections," published in Cist's Advertiser,
some anecdotes of Little Turtle.

Little Turtle was a man of great wit, humor
and vivacity, fond of the company of gentlemen, and delighted in good eating. When I
knew him, he had two wives living with him
under the same roof in the greatest harmony;
one, an old woman, about his own age—fifty
—the choice of his youth, who performed the
drudgery of the house; the other, a young
and beautiful creature of eighteen, who was
his favorite; yet it never was discovered by
any one that the least unkind feeling existed
between them. This distinguished chief died
at Fort Wayne about twenty-five years ago,
of a confirmed case of the gout, brought on
by high living, and was buried with military
honors by the troops of the United States.

The Little Turtle used to entertain us with
many of his war adventures, and would laugh
immoderately at the recital of the following :—
A white man, a prisoner of many years in the
tribe, had often solicited permission to go on a
war party to Kentucky, and had been refused.
It never was the practice with the Indians to

ask or encourage white prisoners among them
to go to war against their countrymen. This
man, however, had so far acquired the confidence of the Indians, and being very impor-
tunate to go to war, the Turtle at length con-
sented, and took him on an expedition into
Kentucky. As was their practice, they had
reconnoitered during the day, and had fixed
on a house recently built and occupied, as the
object to be attacked the next morning a little
before the dawn of day. The house was surrounded by clearing, there being much brush
and fallen timber on the ground. At the appointed time, the Indians, with the white man,
began to move to the attack. At all such
times no talking or noise is to be made. They
crawl along the ground on hands and feet;
all is done by signs from the leader. The
white man all the time was striving to be foremost, the Indians beckoning him to keep back.
In spite of all their efforts he would keep foremost, and having at length got within running
distance of the house, he jumped to his feet
and went with all his speed, shouting at the
top of his voice, Indians! Indians! The Turtle and his party had to make a precipitate
retreat, losing forever their white companion,
and disappointed in their fancied conquest of

the unsuspecting victims of the log cabin. From that day forth this chief would never trust a white man to accompany him again to war.

During the Presidency of Washington, the Little Turtle visited that great and just man at Philadelphia, and during his whole life after, often spoke of the pleasure which that visit afforded him. Kosciusko, the Polish chief, was at the time at Philadelphia, confined by sickness to his lodgings, and hearing of the Indians being in the city, he sent for them, and after an interview of some length, he had his brace of pistols brought forth, and addressing the Chief Turtle, said : I have carried and used these in many a hard fought battle in defense of the oppressed, the weak and wronged of my own race, and I now present them to you with this injunction, that with them you shoot dead the first man that ever comes to subjugate you or despoil you of your country. The pistols were of the best quality and finest manufacture, silver mounted, with gold touch-holes.

CHAPTER III.

JOHN CLEVES SYMMES.

FAR to the East, at Long Island, on the 21st day of July, 1742, a child was born, whose name to-day is second only to that of the United States in the chain of title that connects every home, and all the real estate of this valley with the title paramount vested in the National Grantor.

That John Cleves Symmes, the soldier of the Revolution, a member of Congress, then Chief Justice of the State of New Jersey—should make this purchase, found this settlement, and finally die at Cincinnati, and be buried at North Bend, February 26th, 1814, is a historical romance in which we and our descendants will ever take an increasing interest.

THE MIAMI PURCHASE.

In the winter of 1786–7, Benjamin Stites, of Redstone, Philadelphia, went to New York

for the purpose of obtaining associates with a
view to making a purchase of a large tract of
land, between the two Miamies. He there met
Judge John Cleve Symmes, member of Congress from New Jersey, whose influence he
solicited in making the purchase. Before doing so, Symmes crossed the Alleghanies and
descended the Ohio to its falls. On returning,
the contemplated purchase was made in his
name.

The original contract with Congress called
for a million acres of land, lying between the
Miami rivers, bordering on the Ohio. They
failed in making the required payments, and
the greater part of the tract reverted to the
Government. Symmes, however, obtained a
patent in September, 1794, for 248,540 acres,
for which he paid 66⅔ cents per acre. This constituted the Miami purchase.

GOV. ARTHUR ST. CLAIR.

Much of mournful interest clusters around
this historical figure. The mere mention of
his name always recalls " St. Clair's Defeat,"
sooner than the many distinguished services
rendered his adopted country. The awful
massacre of pioneers at Fort Jefferson, Novem-

ber 4, 1791, by the Indians, called down upon "his gray good head one loud and merciless outcry of abuse, and even detestation. And yet the committee appointed by Congress completely exonerated him from all blame in relation to everything before and during the action."

Few men of his times had larger experience in civil and military affairs, or served the young Republic with more zeal and loyalty, than did General St. Clair. It is our duty to remember the good he did, and forget this one disaster of his otherwise succesful career.

General St. Clair was born in Edinburgh, Scotland, in 1735. He was at first a surgeon in the British Army and crossed the Atlantic in 1759. In our trouble with Great Britian he promptly espoused the cause of the colonies; in 1776 was commissioned colonel, raised a regiment in six weeks, and reported for duty to General Washington. In the same year he was made a brigadier-general, and served as such in the battles of Trenton and Princeton. In 1777 he was appointed major-general and commanded at Ticondoroga. For the surrender of this point, in the face of a greatly superior force commanded by General Burgoyne, he was tried by court-martial and unanimously acquitted. He was restored to his rank and command, served zealously in other parts of the country and closed his Revolutionary career at Yorktown in 1781.

He was a member of the Continental Congress, and chosen President of that body February 2, 1787.

He was our first territorial governor, and was the first citizen of the United States who put in motion the wheels of civil government n the North-west Territory.

He served as governor until 1802, when he returned to his old home in Westmoreland County, Pennsylvania, where he died August 31, 1818, aged 83 years.

He was a man of ability, says Abbott, of fine scholarship and a true gentleman. His patrioism and integrity were unquestioned. His last years were enveloped in gloom, and he died in extreme poverty.

" In May, 1815," said a late writer, " four of us called upon Arthur St. Clair on the top of Chestnut Ridge, eastwardly eight or ten miles from Greensburg, Westmoreland County, Pennsylvania. We were traveling on horseback to Connecticut, and being informed that he kept tavern, we decided to call for entertainment for the night. We alighted at his

residence late in the afternoon, and on entering
the log house we saw an elderly, neat gentleman, dressed in black broad cloth, silk stock-
ings, shining shoes, whose straps were secured by large silver buckles, his hair
clubbed and powdered. On closing his
book he arose and received us most kindly
and gracefully, and pointing us to chairs
he asked us to be seated. On being asked
for entertainment, he said: 'Gentlemen, I
perceive you are traveling and although I
should be gratified by your custom, it is my
duty to inform you I have no hay or grain.
I have good pasture, but if hay or grain are
essential, I cannot furnish them.'

"There stood before us a major-general of
the Revolution—the friend and confident of
Washington—late governor of the territory
North-west of the Ohio River, one of nature's
noblemen, of high, dignified bearing, whom
misfortune, nor the ingratitude of his country,
nor poverty, could break down nor deprive of
self-respect; keeping a tavern in a log house,
but could not furnish a bushel of oats nor a
lock of hay. We were moved principally to
call upon him to hear him converse about the
men of the Revolution and of the North-western
Territory, and our regret that he could not en-

tertain us was greatly increased by hearing
him converse about an hour. The large estate
which he sacrificed for the cause of the Revolution was within a short distance of the top
of Chestnut Ridge—if not in sight."

CHAPTER IV.

CINCINNATI.

THE first settlement between the two
Miamies, was November 18th, 1788, by
Major Stites, who landed opposite the mouth
of the Licking at that time, and began to
erect block houses, as a protection against the
Indians. This settlement was at first called
Columbia. In December following, Colonel
Israel Ludlow, with Denman and Patterson,
left Maysville, Kentucky, with about twenty
persons to commence a settlement on "entire
section 18 and fractional section 17, in township 4," hitherto purchased of Judge Symmes.
During the winter " Mr. Ludlow surveyed and
laid out the town, at that time covered with a
dense forest, blazing the course of the streets
on the trees. This survey embraced only the
portion between Broadway and Western Row
(now Central avenue), and as far north as
Seventh street." Outside of these settlements
the Indians were constantly committing depre-

dations, some of the settlers themselves were
murdered or carried away as captives. To
protect this new enterprise, about the first of
June, 1789, Major Doughty arrived at Losantiville, from Fort Harmar, with 140 men,
and built four block houses on the river bank,
nearly on the site of the present Public Land-
ing. He then laid off a government reservation of fifteen acres, east of Broadway and
south of Fourth street, upon which he erected
Fort Washington; December 29th, General
Harmar arrived with 300 men and assumed
command.

"In February, 1790, Governor St. Clair and
the judges of the Supreme Court of the territory arrived at Losantiville, and organized the
first judicial court in the Miami country. The
governor immediately changed the name of the
place to Cincinnati, erected the County of
Hamilton, and appointed judges of the Court
of Common Pleas, and officers of the militia.
Here he afterward fixed his residence and
built the mansion—a splendid one for its day
—on the corner of Main and Eighth streets,
now in possession of the Western Methodist
Book Concern."

Cincinnati having thus become the seat of
justice, as well as the head-quarters of the

army, began to assume a degree of importance which gave quite the ascendency over the other small towns springing up in the wilderness around it. All the citizens felt that increased importance. It became the centre of rural fashion and refinement.

Ambitious frame houses began to be reared in the place of log huts. Emigrants of intelligence and enterprise were lured to the new emporium. During the summer of 1790, forty log huts were reared, adding very considerably to the grandeur of the town.

CHAPTER V.

THE BATTLE OF FALLEN TIMBERS.

THE victory over the Indians at the battle of Fallen Timbers, upon the Maumee River, in Lucas county, Ohio, August 20, 1794, won by General Wayne, whereby he reclaimed the Country lost by the defeat of General St. Clair, gave peace and its rest and security to this valley. This victory compensated somewhat for the disastrous defeat of the unfortunate St. Clair, denounciation of whom was swallowed up in the victory of Wayne. Then Cincinnati began to lay the foundation for its vast future, the tide of emigration began to swell from its sources in the east. The woodman, no longer apprehensive lest the resounding stroke of the axe should prate of his whereabouts to prowling Indians, cheerily, lustily cleared the forest for his cabin home and garden ground. There are venerable men in our midst to-day —passing away!—whose hearts kindle with warmth when they recall the old fashioned

days of log rollings, the corn huskings, and
the cabin raisings !

"Oft did the harvest to their sickle yield,
   Their furrow oft the stubborn glebe has broke ;
How jocund did they drive their team afield,
   How bowed the woods beneath their sturdy stroke ! ''

Several months after the battle of Fallen
Timbers, a number of Potawatamie Indians
arrived at Fort Wayne, where they expressed
a desire to see " *the Wind*," as they called
General Wayne.   On being asked for an ex-
planation of the name, they replied, that he
was exactly like a hurricane, that drives
and tears everything before it.

General Wayne was a man of the most ardent impulses, and in the heat of action apt
to forget that he was the general—not the
soldier.

When the attack on the Indians, who were
concealed behind the fallen trees was commenced, by ordering the regulars up, General Harrison, then aid to Wayne, being lieutenant with the title of major, addressed his
superior :—" General Wayne, I am afraid you
will get into the fight yourself, and forget to
give me the necessary field orders."   " Perhaps
I may," replied Wayne, " and if I do, recollect

the standing order for the day is, charge the d—d rascals with the bayonet."

GENERAL ANTHONY WAYNE.

This very remarkable man was born in Eastown, Chester County, Philadelphia, January 1st, 1745. He lived not quite fifty-one years. What did he accomplish in his lifetime? We of this valley are so much indebted to this revolutionary hero, that a synopsis of his public services is introduced.

His father was born in Ireland, emigrated to Pennsylvania, 1722; was member of the Provincial Legislature, and was an officer, in early days, in expeditions against the Indians.

Young Wayne received his early education in Philadelphia. His favorite study was mathematics, and for a number of years, was a civil engineer. He was associated with Benjamin Franklin on the "Committee of Safety," touching the welfare of the colonies. At the breaking out of the Colonial troubles, he raised a regiment and was its colonel; in 1777 was promoted to brigadier-general in the Revolutionary Army, and ordered to join General Washington in New Jersey; was at the storming of Stony Point on the Hudson, where he greatly distinguished himself; was in the battles of Yorktown, Monmouth, Brandywine and Germantown, and, indeed, served with distinction until the close of the struggle for Independence. Afterwards he lived awhile in Georgia, being assigned to the command of the army there; was a member of the Constitutional Convention of that State, and served for a short time as a member of the National Congress. In 1792 was appointed by President Washington to the command of the western armies in place of General St. Clair; organized an army, won the battle of Fallen Timbers, dictated the celebrated "Wayne Treaty," August 3, 1795 to the chiefs and warriors of the twelve tribes of Indians east of the Mississippi, and thus conquered and secured peace to the Miami Valley.

Abbott, the historian, says, "that he never received the honors to which he was entitled for his estimable services."

Had he failed in his campaign to recover this valley and to conquer the savages, such scenes of woe, desolation and death would have transpired here as to turn back the tide of emigration for years.

A rare, grand, impetuous military genius; born for the work he so brilliantly accomplished.

"Mad Anthony" Wayne will likewise live forever in the hearts of his countrymen. What Sheridan was to the Shenandoah, Wayne was to the Maimi valley. Of his personal appearance it is said "he was rather above the medium height, his features were regular, and his face decidedly handsome. His dress was scrupulously neat and elegant, his movements were quick, and his manners easy and graceful." He died December 14, 1796, on his way east from Detroit, at Presque Isle, now Erie, Pennsylvania, then a little hamlet in the depths of the wilderness. His dying request was that his body might be buried under the flagstaff of the fort, on the shores of Lake Erie. His body was subsequently removed by his son Colonel Isaac Wayne, in 1809, to Radnor church-yard, near the place of his birth, in Delaware county, Pennsylvania, where an elegant monument stands over his honored dust. Thus, in this world, lived this active, intense heroic man.

His life's campaign closing in martial glory, his brave and loyal soul went out alone on that returnless expedition through the spiritland, for

"There is no death, what seems so is transition ;
    This life of mortal breath
  Is but the suburb of the land elysian
    Whose portal we call death."

CHAPTER VI.

BLOCK HOUSES.

*THE settlement known as White's station was established in 1790. Its particular location, as near as can be described, was where the ice pond now is, north-east of Carthage.

Jacob White, the proprietor of the station, was from Redstone, Pennsylvania. He came to Cincinnati the previous year, and soon afterwards purchased what is now section 1, in Springfield township, and began his improvement as above mentioned. He built a block house, which he occupied with his family.

David Flinn and Andrew Goble each built cabins near the station-house, and the whole were enclosed with a rough log fence. Some time afterwards, perhaps in 1792, Andrew

---

* The accounts of the following stations are given principally in the language of Mr. John G. Olden, taken, by permission, from his "Historical Reminiscences of Hamilton county."

Pryor, Lewis Winans, and John S. Wallace, built cabins on the opposite bank of the creek, within the present limits of the village of Hartwell. And during the same year Moses Pryor and John Riley settled upon a tract of land adjoining White's station on the south. Pryor's tract embraced what is now the County Infirmary farm, in section 6, Mill Creek township, and Mr. Reily's was adjoining on the west, in what is now the north-east corner of section 28, and embraced the site where Carthage was afterwards laid out.

For their natural interest and safety Pryor and Reily agreed to clear and improve their lands jointly. They began by building a cabin and digging a well on Mr. Pryor's tract, at a point about one hundred and fifty yards northeast from the present County Infirmary building. As late as 1875 this old well was yet to be seen, but soon afterwards a few feet of the upper part of the wall was removed, and the well filled up. The land having since been plowed over and cultivated, no traces of it are now left. During the same season Pryor and Reily cleared up and planted a few acres of land.

In the following autumn, Mr. Pryor engaged his services to the government in packing

stores and provisions from Fort Washington
to Fort Hamilton, then the usual mode of
transportation. Two other men were employed with him in the same business, one of
whom was David Flynn, of White's station.
Upon one occasion, after making the trip to
Fort Hamilton in safety, and without molesta-
tion, they started quite early next morning on
their return. On arriving at a little stream,
known since as Pleasant Run, four miles south
of Fort Hamilton, they stopped to refresh
themselves and horses. When about to resume their journey they received a fire from a
body of Indians concealed in the woods. Mr.
Pryor was killed, and the other two men
mounted their horses and made their escape
back to Fort Hamilton. That evening, while
Mrs. Pryor was anxiously awaiting her husband's return to supper, she received the sad
news of his death.

Thus bereaved and left alone with the care
of two small children, she determined to aban-
don, for a time at least, the improvements
her husband had made, and went to reside in
the family of her brother-in-law, Andrew Pryor.
Mr. Reily also gave up his enterprise, returned
to Columbia, and resumed his former occupation of school teaching.

Nothing further of an unusual character occurred to disturb the quiet of this little settlement until the 19th day of October, 1793, when the station was attacked by a band of Indians. Early in the morning of that day a courier stopped at the station, while on his way from Fort St. Clair to Fort Washington, bearing the news of the defeat of Lieutenant Lowry's command, near the former fort. General Wayne, who was then at Fort Jefferson, had sent a small force back to Fort St. Clair, to guard and escort a train of wagons loaded with stores and provisions on its way to Fort Jefferson, and on the 17th day of October, when about 17 miles north of Fort St. Clair, the train was attacked by a large body of Indians. The charge was so sudden and furious that the soldiers became panic stricken and fled without firing a gun, except Lieutenant Lowry and Ensign Boyd, with thirteen non-commissioned officers and privates, who, after a desperate resistance, were all killed. The train was plundered, and sixty-four horses were taken, but the wagons were left standing in the road.

Of this disaster General Wayne thought best to advise the settlements and warn them of danger, and for this purpose the messenger that came to White's station was sent.

A general feeling of security had prevailed throughout the settlements, based upon the supposition that the whole force of the enemy was required to defend their villages along the Maumee and St. Mary's against the invasion of General Wayne. And not even the knowledge that a large band of Indians had thrown themselves in the rear of his army, and were free to advance upon the settlements, was sufficient to fully advise the people of White's station of immediate and imminent danger. The women, it is true, were somewhat alarmed, which caused the men to be more watchful, and remain more closely about the station during the day, thus happily preventing a surprise, and may be a massacre.

Many traditionary accounts have been handed down through the families then belonging to the station concerning the events about to be related as to the battle, differing, as might be expected, as to the details, but the principal facts are well substantiated and may be relied upon as true.

The whole male force about the station at the time consisted of seven men and a boy, viz.: Capt. Jacob White, Andrew Goble, David Flinn, and his two sons Stephen and Benjamin, both full grown men, Andrew

Pryor, Lewis Winans, and Providence, the son of Capt. White, then but ten years of age. John S. Wallace, who resided in a cabin on the north bank of the creek, was at the time on a visit with his family at Cincinnati. The widow of Moses Pryor, with her three children, were residing in the family of her brother-in-law, Andrew Pryor, opposite the station, as before stated.

About five o'clock in the evening the dogs belonging to the station kept up a continuous barking on the hill, not far from the present residence of William R. Morris. Andrew Goble, supposing the dogs had treed a coon proposed to go into the woods and get it, but Capt. White, thinking it possible that there were Indians about, forbade any one going out. Goble, however, persisted, and finally went alone. He had gone but a few hundred yards from the station when he was fired upon and he fell, pierced, as it was afterwards discovered, by a number of balls. The Indians then emerged from their cover (some say, behind the second bank of the creek, others assert that they were concealed in the little ravine, south of where Mr. Morris' residence now stands). They came down the hill with their accustomed war whoop, and as they ap-

36 MILL CREEK VALLEY.

proached the station they observed Mrs. Pryor's
little girl, a child of little more than four years
old, playing upon the opposite bank of the
creek. They at once fired upon it, and it fell
mortally wounded. The mother, who with
her three children were then the only occupants
of the cabins on the north side of the creek,
all the other inmates having gone over to the
station on a visit, heard the firing, and went to
the door of the cabin just in time to witness the
fatal shot that struck her child. Her second
child, a boy between two and three years old,
being sick, she was holding in her arms, while
her babe was lying asleep in the cradle. On
seeing her little girl fall she put down the boy
and went out, under the fire of the Indians,
and bore the child into the house, only however, to find it silent in death.

The savages then opened fire upon the little
block house, which was promptly returned, and
the crack of the rifle was incessant for some
half hour. There were a number of surplus
guns in the station, and the women were kept
busy loading, while the men were thus enabled
to keep up an almost constant fire, making
their number appear much greater. Capt.
White ordered the women to place his hat upon
a pole and run it through the roof of the block

house. This ruse was quite successful for a time in drawing the fire of the enemy.

The Indians, who numbered about thirty, and up to this time were sheltered behind trees at some distance away, now came down the hill upon the station with furious yells, as if to carry it by storm. They were led on by a large and powerful chief, who approached the block-house, and while in the act of scaling the fence, received a fatal shot and fell within the enclosure. The rest of the band seeing their leader fall, retreated back into the woods, where they kept up an occasional fire for an hour or more, and then withdrew and was heard of no more.

In the early part of the engagement several Indians detached themselves from the main body, and, crossing the creek some distance above, came down in the rear of the three cabins on the opposite bank from the station, in one of which Mrs. Pryor and her children resided.

On finding her little girl dead beyond hope, Mrs. Pryor became so distressed over her bereavement that for a time she lost sight of all danger and gave herself up to grief. But the peril was too imminent to allow much time for sorrow. On going to the door of the cabin she saw an Indian approaching but a few hundred yards away, and at once her mind reverted to her surviving children. Her first thought was to grasp both and fly for safety, but a second glance at the Indian warned her that time was precious, and, with a gleam of hope that the savage might spare her babe, she caught up the sick boy and ran with all speed for the station, with the Indian in full pursuit. Without regard to road or ford, she took the most direct course to the block-house, and on coming to the creek sprang into the water up to her waste, crossed the stream, and reached the station in safety, where she was compelled to remain in her wet garments during the night.*

Soon after the attack began Andrew Pryor was dispatched to Fort Washington for aid. He reached the Fort about midnight, and obtained ten dragoons, each bearing an infantry-

*Mrs. Pryor was married in 1794 to Samuel Dunn, and immediately returned to the improvements made by her former husband, on what is now the county infirmary farm. There she and her husband resided for many years and raised a family of six children. Her maiden name was Elizabeth Willis, and was a native of New Jersey. She died on the 2d day of January, 1843, in the 74th year of her age, and was buried in the old Baptist burying ground, at Duck creek. The late Jeremiah Dunn, who resided north of Lockland, was her oldest son.

man behind his saddle, who hastened to the relief of the little station, which they reached about daylight, but found that the Indians had left during the night.

On going to the cabins over the way it was discovered that the savages had taken Mrs. Pryor's babe from the cradle and dashed out its brains against a stump near the cabin door, where its body was found.

They had entered all three of the cabins, ripped open the feather beds, turned out the feathers, and filled the ticks with clothing, coverlets, blankets, household goods, and other valuables, and carried all away. The soldiers followed the trail for several miles, but failed to overtake them.*

During the autumn of 1794, William Moore, who was a great hunter, and who made his

---

* The writer has recently made some inquiry and search for the graves of Andrew Goble and the children of Mrs. Pryor, but there is nothing to mark the tomb of either. Goble, it is said, was buried near the spot where he fell, and the remains of the children were probably placed near his, and this no doubt formed the burial place for the dead of that neighborhood for many years afterwards. A number of tombstones may yet be seen there on the elevated piece of ground east of the canal, a short distance below the acqueduct.

The Indian who fell in the conflict was refused, it is alleged, a christian burial. His body was taken into the woods and given to the fowls of the air, and his bones left to bleach and decay upon the ground.

home at Covalt's station, on the Little Miami river, while out on one of his hunting excursions, wandered to the Great Lick, as it was then called, about a mile and a half east of White's station, and on the lands now owned by John Hamel, in the south-east quarter of section 32. He there killed a deer, which he skinned, and had prepared the saddle for packing, and while in the act of washing his hands in the brook, and at the same time amusing himself by singing an Indian song he had learned while a captive among the Shawnees, he was suddenly alarmed by a voice joining in the song in the Indian tongue. He instantly sprang to his feet and ran for the thick wood on the west, closely pursued by several Indians. As they did not fire they evidently intended capturing him. The foremost runner in the pursuit was quite a small Indian, but very fleet on foot. He was gaining rapidly upon Moore, when, fortunately, they came to a large fallen tree, the body of which was some four feet in diameter. Moore placed his hand upon the log and leaped it at one bound. The Indian, being unable to perform the feat, was compelled to go round the tree. This gave Moore a fresh start, and after a long and closely contested race he reached

White's station, with the loss of his gun and
coat, and also his game.

*GRIFFIN'S STATION.

On the 23d day of July, 1792, Lieutenant
Daniel Griffin entered, in the register's office,
warrant No. 147, and located section 7, T. 3,
E. R. 1, now in Springfield township, and es-
tablished a station or settlement at a point
where the Carthage and Springdale turnpike
row crosses Mill creek, within of the village of
Hartwell, and about half a mile west of White's
station.* Robert Griffin, Daniel and Jacob
Vorhis, Daniel Seward, James McCashen, and
Robert Caldwell and his two sons, Samuel and
James, were among the first settlers.†

*At the time of the attack on White's station by the In-
dians, October 19, 1793, no one resided at Griffin's settlement,
at least no mention is made of any of the settlers or even of
the name of the station in any account or tradition that has
been given of that event. The two stations, measuring in a
direct line, were less than half a mile apart, and it would
seem improbable that persons could have resided within so
short a distance while a battle was in progress without a
knowledge of it, and, in those days, without going to the
relief of their friends. From this it appears quite probable
that Griffin's station was not established until the fall of
1793.

† Some of the descendants of Robert Caldwell are firm in
the opinion that their ancestor settled at Griffin's station as
early as 1790 or '91, but in this they must be mistaken. The

The Griffin brothers built their cabins on the south bank of the creek, as did also Daniel and Jacob Vorhis and Robert Caldwell. Daniel Seward and James McCashen's was at the point where the C. H. & D. railroad now crosses the turnpike. John Winans was also an early settler near this station, but the location of his cabin is not known.

The Caldwells, at an early date, built a saw and grist-mill on the creek, a short distance below the station, and afterwards attached a small distillery. They managed and conducted the entire business until about the year 1806, when a sudden freshet swept the mills away.

TUCKER'S STATION.

In the spring of 1772, a community was organized at Columbia, consisting of Henry and John Tucker,* the brother Luke and Zebulon Foster, Jonathan Pittman, Henry Weaver, and John McCashen.

---

entire section was entered by Daniel Griffin, in July, 1792. The records also show that James Caldwell purchased 446 acres in the section of Lieutenant Griffin, and obtained a deed from Judge Symmes, in 1796. From this the writer is led to believe that no settlement was made at or near where Griffin's and White's stations were built until after July, 1792.

* Henry and John Tucker were both from the Passaic Valley, New Jersey, but were not related, unless very distantly.

They selected section 4, T. 3, entire range 1, now in Springfield township, as their place of settlement, and agreed upon a division of the lands.

They went out into the forest late in the fall of that year, and commenced the erection of a block house and other cabins, at a point on an old Indian trace, known afterwards as Wayne's trace, and still latter as the old Hamilton road. The site selected for the block house was on the east side of the trace, and immediately opposite the late residence of Manning Tucker, son of Henry, the pioneer. The farm is now owned and occupied by Mr. H. Bugher.

Before completing their improvements, a dispute arose between Henry Tucker and Luke Foster as to the division of the lands. Foster, it appears, had paced off and marked his portion according to the plan agreed upon, which gave dissatisfaction to Tucker, who claimed that Foster's line encroached upon the site he had selected for his residence. The dispute became irreconcilable, and Tucker, refusing to have anything further to do with the association, returned to Columbia.

The other parties resumed and had continued their labor for a few days, when Capt. Wells, a spy and Indian hunter, came to their im-

provements, and before they were aware of it
had placed himself between them and their
guns. He did this to admonish them of their
carelessness, and told them they were in imminent danger. He advised them to cease
their labor and return to the settlements on the
Ohio, and await such time as the army, then
organizing under General Wayne, should be
better prepared to protect the interior stations.
The advice of an experienced woodsman, together with the unsettled difficulty existing between Tucker and Foster, induced them to sus-
pend their improvements and return to Columbia.

PLEASANT VALLEY STATION.

During the winter of 1793, Henry Tucker
and the Foster brothers compromised the difficulty before mentioned, Luke Foster agreeing
to accept ten acres in the south-west corner of
the section, and his brother Zebulon, five acres
adjoining the same on the north, in full com-
pensation for their interests in the improvements made on section 4, which, by a new arrangement, was to be divided between Henry
and John Tucker and Jonathan Pittman,
while the Foster brothers, Henry Weaver,
John McCashen, James Seward, and Ziba

Wingent, were to settle on sections 9 and 10,
adjoining on the west.

Under this arrangement they all went out
the following spring to resume their labor and
complete their improvements.

Instead of one they now formed two settlements; but, for mutual safety and protection,
they all joined in the erection of a station-
house at a central point, and convenient to all
the families. The site selected was on the line
between sections 4 and 10, on the west bank
of Mill creek, about where the centre of the
turnpike now is, and near what is still known
as "Station Spring." It was in a beautiful
forest grove, which prompted the settlers to
name it "Pleasant Valley Station."

It was late in the fall, and nearly two months
after General Wayne had started upon his
campaign, that the settlers moved their families out to the station. The army being at
that time in the enemy's country gave confidence and comparative security to the settlements. Neither Tucker's nor Pleasant Valley
stations suffered any serious trouble with the
Indians. No murders or other depredations
were committed, and, save one single incident,
nothing occurred to cause alarm or apprehension of danger. The event referred to, hap-

pened one morning during the winter of 1793-4. Mr. James Seward, while down at the spring getting water, heard what he supposed to be turkeys calling, some distance beyond the creek, and, on going into the station-house, spoke to a Mr. Mahan, who had been about the station for several days, saying : "If you would like to have a turkey, Mahan, I think you can get one if you hurry out, I heard them calling over on the hill." Mahan at once caught up his gun and started in the direction pointed out by Seward. He had gone but a short distance when he heard the peculiar calling of turkeys, and he followed on in that direction until he was led away near a mile from the station, when suddenly a large Indian stepped from behind a tree, not more than twenty yards from him, and said in broken English, "How do," at the same time he saw a gun pointing towards him from a cluster of spice bushes. The surprise was so great and sudden that he dropped his gun and ran with super-human speed for the station, followed closely by the Indians. They no doubt intended capturing him without alarming the settlement, and therefore did not fire upon and kill him at once, as they could easily have done.

When life is at stake, and under the stimulent of fear, men perform feats that seem marvelous and incredible. But such great bodily exertions never fail to expend the vital powers and endanger life. It was so with Mahan; he knew the forfeit should he lose the race, and every nerve and muscle of the body was put to its utmost tension. He outstripped his pursuers and reached the station; but so overcome, that his eyes were protruding and bloodshot. He swooned from exhaustion, and lay for an hour or more in a complete stupor. When reaction came a fever sat in, and for several days his life was despaired of.

CHAPTER VII.

DEATH OF COL. ROB'T ELLIOTT.

IN 1794 Col. Rob't Elliott, contractor for supplying the United States Army, while traveling with his servant from Fort Washington to Fort Hamilton, was waylaid and killed by the Indians at the big hill south of where Thomas Fleming lived, and near the line of Hamilton and Butler counties. When shot he fell from his horse. The servant made his escape by putting his horse to full speed, followed by that of Elliott's into Fort Hamilton.

The savage who shot the colonel, in haste to take his scalp, drew his knife, and seized him by the wig which he wore. To his astonishment the scalp came off at the first touch, when he exclaimed, "dam lie." In a few minutes the surprise of the party was over, and they made themselves merry at the expense of their comrade. The next day a party from the Fort, under the guidance of the servant, visited the spot, placed the body in a coffin and proceeded on their way to Fort Washington. About a mile south of Springdale, they were fired upon by Indians, and the servant, who was on the horse of his late master, was shot at the first fire. The party retreated, leaving the body of Elliott with the savages, who had broken open the coffin, when the former rallied, re-took the body and carried it, with that of the servant to Cincinnati, and buried them side by side, in the Presbyterian Cemetery on Twelfth street.

A WITCH STORY.

About the year 1814, one of our most wealthy and respectable farmers on Mill creek who had taken great pains and expended much money in procuring and propagating a fine breed of horses, was unfortunate in losing a number of them, by a distemper which appeared to be of a novel character. As the disease baffled all his skill, he soon became satisfied that it was the result of witchcraft. Under that impression he consulted such persons as were represented to have knowledge of sorcery, or who pretended to be fortune tellers. These persons instructed him how to proceed to discover and destroy the witch.

One of the experiments he was directed to

make, was to boil certain ingredients, herbs,
etc., over a hot fire, with pins and needles in
the cauldron, which he was told would produce great mental and bodily distress in the
witch or wizard. He tried that experiment,
and while the pot was boiling furiously, placed
himself in his door, which overlooked the principal part of his farm, including the field in
which his horses were kept. It so happened
that, while standing in the door, he saw his
daughter-in-law, who lived in a cabin, about
eighty rods from his own house, hastening to
his spring for a bucket of water. His imagination connected that hurried movement with
his incantation so strongly, that he immediately
ordered his son to move his family from his
farm

From some cause, he had formed an opinion
that a Mrs. Garrison, an aged woman, in feeble
health, fast sinking to the grave, living some
eight or ten miles from his farm, was the principal agent in the destruction of his horses.
He had frequently expressed that opinion in
the neighborhood. Mrs. Garrison had heard
of it, and as might be expected, her feelings
were injured, and here spirits much depressed
by the slanderous report. One of the charms
he had been directed to try, was to shoot a

silver bullet while the witch was evidently in him. This he was told would kill the witch and cure the animals. He accordingly prepared a silver ball and shot it at a very fine brood mare which was affected by the distemper. The mare, of course, was killed; and it so happened, that, in a very short time after, poor Mrs. Garrison died, the experiment was declared to be successful, and the experimenter believed to his death, that his silver bullet killed the poor old woman. However, that may be, his slanderous report had a great effect on her health, and no doubt hastened her death.

CHAPTER VIII.

SPRING IN 1792.

THE winter of 1791-2 was followed by an early and delightful spring. Indeed I have often thought that our western winters were much milder, our springs earlier, and our autumns longer, than they now are. On the last of February some of the trees were putting forth their foliage ; in March, the red bud, the hawthorn, and the dog wood, in full bloom, checkered the hills, displaying their beautiful colors of rose and lily, and in April the ground was covered with May apple, blood root, ginseng, violets and a great variety of herbs and flowers. Flocks of parroquets were seen, decked in their rich plumage of green and gold. Birds of various species, and of every hue were flitting from tree to tree, and the beautiful red bird, and the untaught songster of the West made the woods vocal with their melody. Now might be heard the plaintive wail of the dove, and now the rumbling drum of the partridge, or the loud gobble of the turkey. Here might be heard the clumsy bear, doggedly moving off, or urged by pursuit into a laboring gallop, retreating to his citadel on the top of some lofty tree ; or approached suddenly, raising himself erect in the attitude of defense, facing his enemy and waiting his approach ; then the timid deer, watchfully resting or cautiously feeding or aroused from his thicket, gracefully bounding off, then stopping, erecting his stately head and for a moment gazing around, or snuffing the air to ascertain his enemy, instantly springing off, clearing logs and bushes at a bound and soon distancing his pursuers. It seemed an earthly paradise ; and but for apprehensions of the wily copperhead, who lay silently coiled among the leaves, or beneath the plants, waiting to strike his victim ; the horrid rattlesnake, who more chivalrous, however, with head erect amid its ample folds, prepared to dart upon his foe, generously with the loud noise of his rattle apprised him of danger ; and the still more fearful and invidious savage, who, crawling upon the ground, or noiselessly approaching behind trees and thickets, sped the deadly shaft or fatal bullet, you might have fancied you were in the cofines of Eden or the border of Elysium.—*Indian Captivity, by O. M. Spencer.*

We learn from the old pioneers, that during the early period of the county, the people were in a complete social equality, no aristocratic distinctions were thought of in society, and the first line of demarkation drawn, was to separate the very bad from the general mass. Their parties were for raisings and log rollings, and the labor being finished, their sports usually were shooting and gymnastic exercises with the men, and convivial amusements among the women; no punctilious formality, nor ignobly imitating the fashions of Paris, marred their assemblies, but all were happy and enjoyed themselves in seeing others so. The rich and the poor dressed alike; the men generally wearing hunting shirts and buckskin pants, and the women attired in coarse fabrics produced by their own hands; such was their common and holiday dress; and if a fair damsel wanted a superb dress for her bridal day, her highest aspiration was to obtain a common American cotton check. The latter which now sells for a shilling a yard, then cost one dollar, and five yards was deemed an ample pattern; silks, satins, and fancy goods, that now inflate our vanity and deplete our purses, were not then even dreamed of.

The cabins were furnished in the same style of simplicity; the bedstead was home-made, and often consisted of forked sticks driven into the ground with cross poles to support the clapboards or the cord. One pot, kettle and frying-pan, were the only articles considered indispensable, though some included the tea-kettle; a few plates and dishes upon a shelf in one corner was as satisfactory as is now a cupboard full of china, and their food relished well from a puncheon table. Some of the wealthiest families had a few split bottom chairs, but as a general thing, stools and benches answered the place of lounges and sofas, and at first the green sward or smoothly leveled earth served the double purpose of floor and carpet.

CHAPTER IX.

THE OLD WAYNE ROAD.

IN 1792 a road was projected from Cincinnati up Mill creek by Ludlow's station,
thence to White's station at the third crossing
of Mill creek, and on to Cunningham's and
thence to Runyan's improvement. But back
of this is the fact that this old Wayne road
was at first an Indian trail. It seems to
have been a tribal trait of the Miamies to pass
down the valley over this beaten path to the
Ohio, opposite the mouth of the Licking, thence
crossing into Kentucky. After committing
their depredations they would recross that
river and retread this war path with their
prisoners and plunder.

We will not indulge the imagination in
dwelling upon the scenes of suffering that may
have been enacted along this now crowded
thoroughfare.

Over it passed a portion of the army commanded by General Clark in 1780 ; also the left

wing of General Harmar's army in 1790; a
portion of General St. Clair's in 1791, and that
of General Wayne in 1793.

Over it passed the dead and mutilated body
of Colonel Robert Elliott when borne mourn-
fully back to Fort Washington.

We feel that all this privation and suffering
and death were in some measure a needful
sacrifice on the part of our forefathers in order
that the blessings of christian civilization might
be secured to themselves and their children.

First an Indian trail, narrow and trough-
shaped and tortuous; then a military road,
over which the primitive government trans-
ported troops and stores in its long and bloody
struggle to reclaim this garden from savage
dominion—a rough rude road along which
the iron six-pounder floundered, and over
which

"In their ragged regimentals
Marched the old Continentals."

Then it loudened into a great highway
along which to-day pours a continuous tide of
humanity, but resounding no more to the tramp
of mustering squadrons or the rumble and the
grumble of artillery.

It is an exceedingly interesting fact that Mr.

David D. Mills, the father of Joseph F. Mills,
Esq., the proprietor of Maplewood, was one of
General Wayne's soldiers, and marched along
this old road, uninformed as an old Continental,
on that celebrated campaign and took a con-
spicious part in the battle of Fallen Timbers.

In reference to Wayne's campaign, Mr.
Olden says :—

"General Wayne left Camp Hobson's
Choice, at Cincinati, on the 7th day of October 1793, and followed the general course of
the old track running along the Mill Creek
valley and which had previously been opened
as a *great road* as far as White's station. He
camped for the night on the grounds lately occupied as a race course, and known as the
Buckeye Club grounds, near the present village of Elmwood. The following day he
passed through White's station, and along
what is now Wayne Avenue, through Maplewood and Lockland ; thence through Tucker's
station, and where the town of Springdale now
is, to Fort Hamilton, where he encamped the
second night."

AN INDIAN BATTLE.

Tradition has it that a battle was fought

between hostile Indian tribes in this valley, just above White's station, about the year 1780.

The legend is traced back directly to old Capt. White. It may be deemed "a legend, a phantom, a show," but that sturdy old pioneer, told Wm. R. Morris, deceased, (the father of Wm. R. Morris, Esq., who now resides on the bluff overlooking this spot,) that when he first came to build White's station, Indian bones were thickly scattered over the ground, intermingled with battle axes, arrows, and other implements of savage warfare. About four thousand were believed to have been engaged.

> "Lo! how all things fade and perish;
> From the memory of the old men
> Pass away the great traditions,
> Perish in the ears that hear them.
> Do not reach the generations
> That, as yet unborn, are waiting
> In the great mysterious darkness
> Of the speechless days that shall be."

AN OLD GRIST MILL.

Just above White's station, on the banks of Mill creek, there once stood an old grist mill. It was built about the year 1795 by Capt. White. Every trace of it is now gone, save

the excavated spot where it stood suggestive
of its rude foundations. Old trees stand round
about it, as if erected by the hand of nature
in memory of the good it did in departed years.

You can still see the sunken grass-covered
mill-race that leads down from the old dam that
diverted the waters from their natural to this
artificial channel. The hands that dug it,
where are they?

> Oh, earth!
> Where are the past?
> And wherefore had they birth?
> The dead are thy inheritors—and we
> But bubbles on the surface, and the key
> Of thy profundity is in the grave.

But the voice of the miller is hushed; the
sound of the grinding has died into an echo;
the water goes unvexed to the sea, while the
old water-wheel revolves only in the realm of
the imagination.

It stood as a sort of Pioneer Exchange, until
1827, when, mainly by reason of the construction of the canal, it fell into disuse and was
shortly afterwards succeeded by what is now
known as the Palmer Flour Mills of Lockland,
into the hoppers of which pour the grain from
the same fields cleared and tilled by the pion-

eers as patrons of the old White Mill, and from which issue one hundred and fifty barrels of flour per day the year round.

BLOODY RUN.

*John Ludlow, who was a native of New Jersey, and a half brother to Israel, the surveyor, came to Cincinnati in November, 1796, and was the first acting sheriff of Hamilton county.

In the spring of 1794, Mr. Ludlow moved out upon a tract of land which he had previously purchased in section 17, T. 3. F. R. 2, now in Mill Creek township. His cabins were built on the east side of Mill creek, a short distance south of the lands lately used as a trotting course. The particular site was where the old frame dwelling, known as the Ludlow homestead, now stands.

Moving into the interior of the forest, even at that late period of the Indian war, was not regarded entirely free from danger; and Mr. Ludlow very prudently joined the company of a few families who were moving out to White's station. Captain Jacob White, who was then

---

*Mr. Olden's Sketches.

in Cincinnati, rode with the company also, it
being on his way home. And Thomas Goudy
(who was the first practicing lawyer in Cincinnati), with two young women, Abby Coch-
rane and Sarah Freeman, went along with the
company on horseback as a mere pleasure ex-
cursion.

They reached Ludlow's cabins without en-
countering any trouble, and Captain White and
his party moved on toward their destination.

The road from Ludlow's improvement to
White's station had been opened and traveled
for several years previous, and formed a part
of the great highway leading from Fort Washington to Fort Hamilton, over which had been
wagoned or packed all the supplies and muni-
tions for Wayne's army. Along this road
White's party, including Goudy and the two
young women, had proceeded not more than
half a mile when they heard a volley of mus-
ketry but a short distance up the road. They
knew from the almost simultaneous discharge
of the guns that the firing did not proceed
from hunters, and at once suspected that the
Indians were engaged in some work of death.
The whole party were alarmed, and some
were excited with fear. Captain White, who
was experienced in Indian warfare, having

been raised on the borders of Pennsylvania, endeavored in vain to rally them. They returned in confusion to Ludlow's cabins, where they all came to a halt except lawyer Goudy and the two young ladies, who continued their flight down the road to Cincinnati. Captain White determined to remain upon the ground for a time and await further events. It was not long until two men on horseback came dashing down the road. They proved to be pack-horsmen, in the government service, and from them he learned that the firing was indeed an affair of death. There were four of these men in company, who, while stopping at a little stream beyond to give their horses drink, received a volley from a small band of Indians concealed by the road side. One of their number fell instantly killed, another was severely, and a third slightly wounded. On learning this grave news, Captain White speedily returned to Ludlow's improve· ment, accompanied by the two men, one of whom was slightly wounded. There he procured a sufficient force and started in pursuit of the savages. They were not successful in overtaking them, however, but they found the body of the man that was killed, and buried him near the spot where he fell. They also found and took charge of the other soldier who was severely wounded, and sent him to Ludlow's station (now Cumminsville), where he was left at the house of Abner Boston, and where, after lingering for several days, he died. This event gave the name of Bloody Run to the little stream where it occurred, which it still retains.

In 1857, the late Solomon Burkhalter (who died in Reading but a few years since), while engaged in building a new bridge over Bloody Run, dug up the remains of the poor fellow who, sixty-three years before, had fallen there. Not knowing what else to do, Mr. Burkhalter placed the bones deeper in the earth, beneath the abutment, where all that is left of this unknown soldier still remains.

THE OLD BURYING GROUND.

South of the aqueduct at Carthage, upon a little knoll overlooking the villages beneath it, is an object of peculiar interest.

Once so lonely in its wilderness seclusion, now an open, conspicuous, and sunny spot on the margin of the canal; so near as to tremble at passing railroad trains; molested by the " secular confusions " of the fair grounds, but undisturbed by the spirit-like communications carried on over the telegraphic and telephonic wires stretched almost immediately above this "noiseless suburb of the land Elysian." Let us enter there. The graves cannot be counted; not because they are numberless, but because nature's hand has smoothed the many "mouldering heaps" down to the level of the earth, and covered and concealed the dreamless ones, so that no evidence whatever remains to show that the green sod had ever been broken for the sepulture of the dead. Some graves are yet marked by the still protruding head or foot-stone, but they, too, seem to seek obscurity underneath the ground. Only a few, distinguishable by a simple monument.

On a mouldering stone we read:
"EDWARD WHITE, The 2d.
Born 1746. Died 1798."
Born in England, died on the American frontier! What sought he and his silent partners thus afar? Out on the skirmish line of advancing civilization, they fell early on the ground where the battle was finally fought and won.

Here were buried Andrew Goble, and two of Mrs. Pryor's children, who were

killed by the Indians at the time of the battle
at White's station. Here also sleep two of the
Rudolphs, uncle and cousin to Mrs. Lucretia
R. wife of the lamented GARFIELD.

After their toil and struggles and privations,
after their homely joys and enduring triumphs,
they sleep well. Do they sleep?

> " These under-earth inhabitants—are they
> But mingled millions decomposed to clay ?
> Or do they in their silent cities dwell,
> Each in his incommunicative cell ?

CLIMATE NINETY YEARS AGO.

The Ohio and Scioto companies, in order
to induce immigration, sent Joel Barlow to
Europe for this purpose.

He described to the toiling denizens of
Paris, the new world to which they were invited,
in the following language :—

" The climate of Ohio is wholesome and delightful. Fruit, even in winter, is almost entirely unknown. The river, called by way of
eminence, ' The Beautiful' abounds in excel-
lent fish of a vast size. There are noble
forests, consisting of trees which spontaneously
produce sugar. There is a plant which yields
ready-made candles. There is venison in

plenty, the pursuit of which is uninterrupted
by wolves, foxes, lions or tigers. A couple of
swine will multiply themselves a hundred fold
in two or three years, without taking any care
of them. There are no taxes to pay and no
military service to be performed."
This *might* have been so then ; but if so,
how changed!

INDIAN SUMMER.

We obtain an idea of Indian summer,
such as the early settlers saw, from a description of this remarkable season of the year
found in Drake's "Pictures of Cincinnati
in 1815."

" It began in October and November, and
continued generally two or three weeks with
occasional storms. The atmosphere was, for
the most part, dry, serene, and smoky, through
which the sun and moon, in the morning and
evening, exhibited a face of darkened crimson.
The verdure of the forest faded away or passed
into the cloudless varieties of brown, red and
yellow, which gave to the surrounding scenery
a dull and sombre aspect."

The cause of the smokiness was supposed
to be conflagrations by the Indians of withered

grass and herbs in the extensive prairies of the North-west.

"Apollo still our long, long summer gilds,"

But the mellow days of the Indian summer seem to have departed with the red man, to return no more; at least such as were seen by our forefathers, a half a hundred years ago.

> "From gold to gray
> Our mild sweet day
> Of Indian summer fades too soon;
> But tenderly
> Above the sea
> Hangs, white and calm, the hunter's moon."
> *John Greenleaf Whittier.*

SIGNIFICANCE AND ORIGIN OF THE NAME OHIO.

Kis-ke-pi-la-sepe, *i. e.,* Eagle river, was the name given to the Ohio river by the Shawanoese. But the Wyandots, who were in this country generations before the Shawanoese, called it *O, he, zuh.* This is regarded as the primitive name and means, "great, grand and fair to look upon." The French voyagers used this name in their boat songs—adopting its signification when they called it *La Belle Riviere.*

> "Romantick is Ohio's stream,
> Through wild woods wandering, deep, and slow,
> While on its waveless mirror seen
> Cliffs, trees, and clouds, inverted glow.
> CINCINNATI, 1829.   *N. Guilford.*

CHAPTER X.

HAMILTON COUNTY

A S at first organized, included about one-eighth of the present area of Ohio.

Clermont, Warren, Butler, Preble, Montgomery, Greene, Clinton, Champaign, Miami and Drake counties were formed out of it.

It embraces at present about 390 square miles, or 249 thousand acres.

It is bounded on the south by the Ohio river; on the west by Dearborn county, Indiana; on the north by Butler and Warren counties, and on the east by the Little Miami river.

It was named " Hamilton " county by Governor St. Clair, in honor of Alexander Hamilton, then Secretary of the United States Treasury.

The population of the county in 1880 was 313,870.

SPRINGFIELD TOWNSHIP

Was organized in 1795. It now contains

forty-two sections, some of them being ·less
than full size, and containing twenty-five
thousand eight hundred and ninety-six acres,
and, next to Sycamore township, is the largest
in the county.

It is bounded on the north by Butler county,
on the west by Coleran, on the south by Mill
creek and on he east by Sycamore township.
The eastern part of it is in Mill Creek valley.
The east and west forks of Mill creek unite in
this township, and which, with their tributaries,
render it a well watered region.

The Cincinnati, Hamilton and Dayton railroad runs through the eastern part ; the Dayton Short Line, through the north-east corner ;
the College Hill road has two miles of track
laid in the south-western part. The Cincinnati,
Avondale, Glendale and Hamilton narrow
guage is projected to form a junction with the
Cincinnati Northern upon whose track it seeks to
enter the city.

· The old Hamilton turnpike passes through
it from north to south. The old Wayne war
trace is now an avenue through Carthage, Hartwell, Maplewood, Lockland, Woodlawn, to
Glendale, Springdale and Hamilton ; also the
Winton road or pike affords traveling accommo-
dations. The Lebanon pike touches the south-

east corner. The Miami canal traverses it about two miles.

The remains of the Mound Builders are found in this township. Mr. Olden says:—

A number of mounds and other ancient relics have been discovered in Springfield and Sycamore townships. There is a small mound on the Readinbo farm (now belonging to the estate of Dr. Wright). It is of the ordinary conical shape, at present seventy-five feet in diameter, and seven to eight feet high; having been plowed over for many years, its height is greatly reduced. Another of more singular construction is situated on the lands formerly belonging to Price Thompson. It consists of a circular excavation, 500 feet in circumference, with an embankment on the outer circle, which originally must have been twelve to fif-teen feet high, measuring from the bottom of the excavation. In the centre of this circle is a conical shaped mound, raised as high, or perhaps to a greater height than the outer embankment. The many centuries of rains and the recent cultivation of the lands have greatly marred the shape and former appearance of this work. The writer remembers it fifty years ago, then much more distinct and prominent. Its outlines, however, are still plainly traceable.

On the farm of Mr. James Shepherd, adjoining Lockland, is a small mound, forty feet in diameter at the base, five feet high, and of oval shape. About two hundred yards east, and on the lands of Mr. Francis Pentland, is an excavation from which there is little doubt the earth was taken that forms the mound. A few years ago Mr. Shepherd dug into it and found at its centre base a heap of ashes and charcoal, but nothing more.

Another small mound, about the same dimensions as the last described, except that it is one foot higher, is situated in section 4, Springfield township, on the lands of Noah Babs.

One, larger than either of the two last mentioned, is on the farm now owned by Maynard French, in section 11, Springfield township, south of Glendale. It is seventy-three feet in diameter north and south, and sixty-three feet east and west, at the base, with an altitude of eight feet. It is covered with forest trees, oak and ash, some of which are more than twenty inches in diameter. Some persons in digging into it years ago, left two uneven and ill-looking depressions, which mar the appearance of this otherwise beautiful little mound."

As a theatre of war, it may be stated, that it has resounded to the tread of armed men;

a portion of General Clark's forces in 1780, and the left wing of General Harmar's army in 1791, passed through it on the way to chastise the Indians of the Miami valley ; the armies of St. Clair and Wayne crossed and recrossed it ; the rebels, under the command of General John H. Morgan, passed through Springdale and Glendale in 1863, and General Hobson, commanding the union forces, in pursuit.

Dr. Drake in his " Pictures of Cincinnati," says : " In 1810, Springfield township had nearly 58 inhabitants to each square mile, and could certainly support many more."

It is now populous and wealthy. Its farm lands are rich and highly improved. Some of the principal suburbs of Cincinnati are in it— Glendale, Springdale, Woodlawn, Park Place, Wyoming, Lockland, Maplewood, Hartwell, and North Carthage.

Its tax duplicate in 1880, exclusive of incorporated villages, was $2,907,834, and its population was 7,979.

MILL CREEK VALLEY

Comprises the following political divisions : That part of Cincinnati township lying immediately on each side of Mill creek at its

entrance into the Ohio river, Mill Creek
township, Springfield township, and the western part of Sycamore township.

It extends from the Ohio river to the Great
Miami river bed at Hamilton.

In Judge Burnet's note on the North-west
territory we read, that

"Those who are acquainted with Mill Creek
valley know that it is connected with the Great
Miami in the neighborhood of Hamilton, and
that there is now a large pond near that
place, about twenty miles from Cincinnati,
from which, in wet seasons, the water passes
through Pleasant Run into the Miami below
Hamilton, and by Mill creek into the Ohio at
Cincinnati.

Geologists claim that nothing but drift terraces, that make the walls of the present course
of the Big Miami, shut out that stream from
entering the Ohio river where Mill creek now
enters it, and assert that there is the best reason for believing that the Great Miami at one
time did pursue this valley, or ancient river
bed, to the Ohio, and furthermore, speak of it
now as "a deep and wide valley traversed by
an insignificent stream, wholly inadequate to
account for the erosion of which it has availed
itself."

There was a time, it is asserted, when there was no valley here, or rather, no hills in Hamilton county. They are merely the isolated remnants of the old plateau which so long and so far have resisted the slow process of denudation. This valley is the result of that erosion.

A scholarly gentleman * passing through Mill Creek valley, noticed the remarkable geological formation exposed by the cut made by the railroad just above the Maplewood depot in the southern part of Wyoming. He wrote a learned paper accounting for it on geological principles. From it we gather important and reliable information. He asserts that "at one time this valley did not exist; that the country from the Little to the Big Miami was a dead level." This was when the earth was young, approaching maturity through the glacial period. He theorizes "that an immense mountain of ice and snow found its way from far northern regions to the southward, until its southern base reached to the Ohio river and perhaps beyond, and extended back as far as Glendale." This enormous weight ploughed out this valley, leaving the hills standing because of their being filled

* Prof. Florien Giauque, of the Cincinnati Bar.

with stone, which resisted glacial action while the soft intermediate earth yielded.

Under the action of the sun, "through the still lapse of ages," this ice mountain finally melted, and, the water running to the sea left a residuum of gravel and sand and soil. From this sprang the forests and vegetation which shadowed the valley and enriched it with their deciduous leaves; then came the green pastures beside the still waters, and the abounding game,—in its pristine beauty, the whilom habitation of pre-historic man, who cast up the mute, mysterious mound, buried his dead and departed forever; then the happy hunting ground of the Indian, who loved it as his wildwood home, and in defense of which many and many a warrior has died before the white man forced his way across its verdant threshold.

> Ye say they all have passed away,
> That noble race and brave;
> That their light canoes have vanished
> From off the crested wave;
> That 'mid the forests where they roamed
> There rings no hunter shout;
> But their names are on your waters,
> Ye may not wash it out.

Then came the pioneers and transformed it

into farm lands. To-day it is an amphi-theatre
where may be heard and seen the hum and
crowd and shock of men in a great civic tourn-
ament which will be continued, with increasing
attractions,

"To-morrow, and to-morrow, and to-morrow
To the last syllable of recorded time."

MILL CREEK OR MAH-KE-TE-WAH

Is an ancient water course. The east branch
brings us water from Butler county ; the west

" From sources which well
In the tarn on the fell "

in the broken uplands of Colerain township.
These two branches become united in one
stream at Hartwell, and then journey together
to the sea. How gleefully they turned the old-
fashioned water wheels of the grist-mills in the
reclaimless past! How famous and prolific
the fishing pools! Before the woods upon its
margin bowed to the axe of the pioneer, how
cool and inviting its banks!

Its waters have refreshed the hunter when in
pursuit of game or pursued by the savage.

Here the wounded stag has cooled his
swollen tongue,

> That from the hunter's aim
> Had ta'en a hurt and come to languish,
> And the big round tears coursed
> One another down his innocent nose
> In piteous chase, and stood on the
> Extreme verge of the swift brook
> Augmenting it with tears.

All this before Lockland became the little manufacturing city that it is—and, together with the lower Villages, Infimaries, Factories, etc. on its banks, converted Mill creek into little less, at times, than an open Parisian sewer—suggesting that described by *Victor Hugo* in which Jean Valjean found himself—"on all sides putridity and miasma, and here and there a trap through which Villon inside converses with Rabelais outside."

Ma-ke-te-wa is supposed to be the Indian name for Mill creek. This, however, is *but* a supposition. It is not a tradition. And yet it has been called that by poets and authors for over fifty years.

William D. Gallagher, the Pioneer of Western poets, has immortalized this little stream in the following beautiful poem:—

THE SPOTTED FAWN.

On Maketewa's flowery marge
  The red chief's wigwam stood,
When first the white man's rifle rang
  Loud through the echoing wood ;
The tomahawk and scalping knife
  Together lay at rest—
For peace was in the forest shades,
  And in the red man's breast.

      Oh, the spotted fawn !
      Oh, the spotted fawn !
  The light and the life of the forest shades
    With the red chief's child is gone !

By Maketewa's flowery marge
  The Spotted Fawn had birth,
And grew, as fair an Indian girl
  As ever blessed the earth ;
She was the red chief's only child,
  And sought by many a brave,
But to the gallant young White Cloud
  Her plighted troth she gave.

      Oh, the Spotted Fawn ! &c.

From Maketewa's flowery marge
  Her bridal song arose;
None dreaming, on that festal night,
  Of near encircling foes ;
But through the forests, stealthily,
  The white men came in wrath ;
And fiery deaths before them sped,
  And blood was in their path.

      Oh, the Spotted Fawn, &c,

On Maketewa's flowery marge
  Next morn, no strife was seen ;
But a wail went up were the young Fawn's blood
  And White Cloud's dyed the green,
And burial in their own rude way
  The Indians gave them there,
While a low and sweet-toned requiem
  The brooks sang, and the air.

          Oh, the Spotted Fawn !
          Oh, the Spotted Fawn !
        The light and life of the forest shades
        With the red chief's child is gone.

CINCINNATI, December, 1844.

"THE SPOTTED FROG."

A parody on the " Spotted Fawn," soon
after appeared, which created a sensation and
became the rage for awhile. The authorship
remained a long time a mystery. But now it
is widely known, that Lewis J. Cist, Esq., a
literary pioneer of the west, is its gifted and
distinguished author. We here insert it :—

On muddy Mill creek's marshy marge,
  When summer's heat was felt,
Full many a burly bullfrog large
  And tender tadpole dwelt,
And there at noondays, might be seen,

Upon a rotted log;
The bullfrogs brown and tadpoles green,
    And there the spotted frog.
        Oh, the spotted frog!
        Oh, the spotted frog!
The light and life of Mill creek's mud
    Was the lovely spotted frog!

By stagnant Mill creek's muddy marge
    The spotted frog had birth,
And grew as fair and fat a frog
    As ever hopped on earth;
She was the frog chief's only child,
    And sought by many a frog;
But only upon one she smiled,
    From that old rotted log.
        Oh, the spotted frog! &c.

From muddy Mill creek's stagnant marge
    Her bridal song arose,
None dreaming, as they hopped about,
    Of near encircling foes;
But cruel boys in search of sport,
    To Mill creek came that day,
And at the frogs with sticks and stones
    Began to blaze away!
        Oh, the spotted frog! &c.

On marshy Mill creek's muddy marge,
    Next morn, no frogs were seen;
But a mortal pile of sticks and stones
    Told where the fray had been;
And time rolled on, and other frogs
    Assembled 'round that log,

But never Mill creek's marshes saw
Again that spotted frog !
Oh, the spotted frog !
Oh, the spotted frog !
The light and life of Mill creek's mud
Was the lovely spotted frog !

CINCINNATI, January, 1845.

A PIONEER'S POEM.

The following affectionate apostrophe to
Mill creek, was written by one born upon its
banks more than sixty years ago.

Only communion with its running waters in
its earlier days, could have inspired such a
pretty pastoral poem—a rural picture and story
—the sentiment of which is both beautiful and
ennobling.

Its modest author is rightly supposed to be
John G. Olden, Esq., whose "Historical
Sketches, etc. in Hamilton county" have
been of valuable assistance to the writer ; grateful acknowledgments for which are here and
now made.

TO MILL CREEK.

Thou rude little stream, so modest in mien,
And flowing so quietly by,
No white pebbled floor or rock mantled shore,
Nor cliffs mounting rugged and high.

No dark lurid dells, or deep hidden cells,
　My reverence or awe to inspire,
No pomp or display in coursing thy way,
　Nor aught for the world to admire.

Yet dearer to me than Niagara,
　Or all the bright rivers of earth,
For a spot I descry thy waters near by,
　Marked out as the place of my birth.

Oh, the scenes lying near, to memory how dear,
　And incidents blended with thee!
The brooks and the rills, the valleys and hills,
　Have each a charmed legend for me.

'Twas there in the glades and deep forest shades,
　My happiest moments were spent,
Unburdened with care and free as the air,
　A rustic young monarch I went.

There I plucked the black haw and yellow paw-paw,
　The mulberry purple and red,
The juicy wild plum and blue grapes that hung
　In clusters just over my head.

When summer had come in verdure and bloom,
　With other young truants I ran
Along the green banks with merry wild pranks,
　And oft in thy waters we swam.

We climbed for the nest of the robin redbreast,
　Threw stones at the blackbird and wren,
We drove the young thrush from her nest in the bush,
　The chipmonk we chased to her den.

Unheeding the sign, with hook and the line
   We angled thy waters for bass,
Yet ever content if homeward we went
   With shiners enough for a mess.

At night's darkest hue the coon to pursue,
   The hounds from the kennel we take ;
And away we all go with a wild " Tally-ho ! "
   Through tanglewood, marshes and brake.

A bleak tempest-blast, brings winter at last
   And robes the earth over in snow,
The rabbit we trail—we're trapping the quail,
   Or down the hill coasting we go.

Again, at a time in my youthful prime,
   With a witching young friend I strayed ;
While roaming thy shores to pluck the wild flow'rs,
   Our secrets to each we betrayed.

'Twas there in the shade that the sycamore made,
   The redbird sang sweetly above,
Through mystical charms that beauty adorns,
   My heart beat responsive to love.

Where wild lilies grew and violets blue,
   And buttercups gaily arrayed,
Mid the fragrant perfume of the may-apple bloom,
   Our vows to each other we made.

But oh ! fleeting Time, with ruthless design,
   Had wrought many changes since then,
His magical wand had swept the woodland,
   And furrowed the faces of men.

Beneath the green sward in the old church-yard,
    Are silently lying at rest
The dearest of friends, whose pale, spectral hands,
    Wave back through the shadowy mist.

All passing away, my locks they are gray,
    And life is now ebbing with me,
Yet remember dear stream, in the land of my dream
    I'll be singing bright peans to thee.

CHAPTER XI.

BRIDGES.

UPON this subject Dr. Drake* said : "Some enthusiastic persons already speak of building a bridge across the Ohio, at Cincinnati, but the period at which this great project can be accomplished is certainly remote," and

" There was a bridge over Mill creek, near its confluence with the Ohio ; but in consequence of a high flood in that river it was destroyed."

It is an astonishing fact, with which we are too familiar to fully realize it, that two immense iron railroad bridges, and one of the finest suspension bridges in the world, connect the States of Ohio and Kentucky, and beneath which the wrinkled river seems at times to crawl.

Many—some of them costly and beautiful— are the bridges that now span the Mill creek.

---

* Pictures of Cincinnati, 1815.

But the most suggestive sight of the kind is afforded at what was known in early days as "The third crossing of Mill creek," just above Carthage.

These five bridges have been constructed since the nineteenth day of [October, 1793, when Mrs. Andrew Pryor, regardless even of the old ford, sprang into the water up to her waist and escaped with her child across Mill creek to avoid captivity and murder by the Indians, as stated under the head of " White's station."

We have at first an old rude bridge on the Hamilton pike ; then the aqueduct for the canal ; then the bridge on the C. H. & D. R. R. ; then that on the Dayton Short Line ; and finally the new iron bridge on Wayne avenue. These have been necessitated by the ever widening stream of population, and the ever increasing volume of trade and traffic through this valley—the richest and most populous in Ohio —in the west.

THE CALDWELL HOMESTEAD.

This valuable landed estate belongs at present to Col. James N. Caldwell, U. S. A. upon which he resides with his family. His title is derived from the last will and testament of his uncle, Major James Caldwell, who purchased and obtained a deed in 1796 directly from Judge Symmes for the 446 acres of which it consists.

Major Caldwell was one of the earliest pioneers of this valley. He was commissioned major by General Wayne and commanded a regiment upon Wayne's expedition against the Indians and was at the battle of Fallen Timbers. He was a distinguished continental soldier, served his country faithfully and continuously until peace was declared with the Indians, when he purchased this body of land out of his earnings—a monument as well to his frugality as to his loyalty.

Mill creek passes almost through the center of it from north to south, the eastern portion being in the corporation of Carthage, the western consisting of a natural forest.

Griffin's station was located near this farm at an early day, an account of which appears on page 41.

Soon after this purchase, the Caldwells built a saw and grist-mill on the creek just west of the station. This was the first mill built on Mill creek, and it is asserted upon good authority, was the first in the Miami valley.   Judge

Symmes built a house at North Bend out of timber sawed in this mill, which was hauled by ox-teams over the old road still leading west from Carthage and known as the North Bend road.

A distillery was also built and put in operation on the west bank of Mill creek at the mouth of one of the ravines on this farm. What its spirit producing capacity was, is not known. It is known, however, that it was the beginning of that vast distilling interest from which the Government derives at present a yearly revenue of nearly $12,000,000 from this valley. A sudden storm swept it out of existence in 1806.

The copper still—doubtless the first brought to this valley from Philadelphia—was subsequently found among drift wood and came, somehow, into the possession of a criminal accused of stealing a horse. The head of a now wealthy and distinguished family —then a lawyer—defended and acquitted the man and for his fee took the copper still. The lawyer traded it subsequently for ninety acres of ground, which was the beginning of the largest and richest landed estate in Hamilton County.

The Caldwells are direct descendants of

Robert Caldwell a compatriot of Judge Symmes, and grandfather to Col. Caldwell of Carthage, and the Hon. John W. Caldwell, of the Cincinnati Bar, formerly U. S. Minister to Bogota.

THE MIAMI CANAL

Is an interesting and by no means unimportant feature of this valley. It affords substantial advantages to manufacturers; cheap and safe transportation; and pleasurable advantages by way of skating and piscatorial amusement in their respective seasons. It provides a safe bathing beach for boys and dogs, for there need be no apprehension of the ebb and flow of the tides, or of counter currents, or sharks.

In its ceaseless flow it suggests the song of Tennyson's brook:

> " By thirty mills I hurry down,
>   Or slip between the ridges,
>   By twenty thorps, a pretty town,
>   And half a hundred bridges;
>   And draw them all along and flow,
>   To join the brimming river,
>   For men may come and men may go,
>   But I go on forever."

The Tiber rolls in splendor through Rome;

this moves in majesty through Carthage.
Like the " Beautiful Blue Danube " it forms
the boundaries of cities, and flows through a
valley alike famous for its natural scenery and
magnificent residences. It resembles the Seine in that its placid
waters reflect the domes and minarets of the
Paris of America, although the ashes of Na-
poleon do not sleep upon its banks.

It has a " Bridge of Sighs." Happy lovers
have realized this fact while standing upon
it in the deepening twilight and the brightening
moonlight, as they listened to " the light
drip of the suspended oar," or mused as the
Lockland Packet passed along this Venetian
avenue.—

" This quiet sail is as a noiseless wing
To waft me from distraction ; once I loved
Torn ocean's roar, but thy soft murmuring
Sounds sweet as if a sister's voice reproved."

It might as well be subjoined as a practical,
historical fact, that this Canal was excavated
and formally opened, A. D. 1827. A meeting
was held at the Locks—from which Lockland
derives its name—at which Gov. DeWitt
Clinton of New York, made the speech of
dedication. Its construction was a marvelous
event in its day. The time is believed to be

rapidly approaching, when its channel through
the valley will be usurped by railroads.

SPRING GROVE CEMETERY.

The old White burying ground at Carthage,
elsewhere mentioned, and other homely resting places for our departed fore-fathers, have
been supplanted, in the main, by this magnificent city of the dead. And much of the wide-
spread celebrity of Mill Creek valley is attributable to the fact that this Cemetery is located
within it.

We find in Kenny's Illustrated Cincinnati,
a description of it so complete and satisfactory,
that by permission we here insert it.

"The organization of the owners of the Cemetery of Spring Grove was begun on the 14th
of April, 1844, when a number of the leading
citizens of Cincinnati assembled, and appointed
a committee to select a site. The old Garrad
farm, of 160 acres, was chosen, and on the 21st
of January following, the Society was incorporated. To place it upon a firm basis, two
hundred citizens subscribed one hundred dollars each, for which they were entitled to select
a lot fifty feet square. In February, 1845, in
memory of the springs and groves, the farm

was named Spring Grove, and consecrated on the 28th day of August, in the same year. The original design for the improvement of the ground was prepared by the late Mr. John Notman, who also planned Laurel Hill Cemetery, near Philadelphia; but the chief, and most characteristic improvements have been made since 1855. It is from this period that the present lawn-landcape style date; and within all the hedges and iron and stone inclosures have been removed. Its green slopes and wooded levels, its stately avenues and beautiful monuments, shrubberies and flowers, now form component parts of one great whole, unobstructed by fences, and diversified by quiet lakes. To the original purchase, 434 acres have been added, at a cost of $330,000, thus forming at once a peaceful resting place for 'the dead, and a beautiful park for the living.

In the Old World two of the most famous and largest cemeteries are the Pere la Chaise, in France, and the Groves at Scutari, where the remains of tens of thousands of Mussulmans lie buried. These are now part and parcel of history, for they have entomed many generations. The simple tomb so recently repaired, where Abelard and Eloise sleep together, is one of the shrines of Pere la Chaise. Upon the anniversary of the funeral, thousands and thousands of Parisians flock to the spot to garland it with flowers and crowns of immortelles.

The curators of the grounds say that the grave of these lovers is almost the only one which has been visited and mourned over and decorated with unvarying constancy during all the procession of years. Scores of Frenchman have told the tale of their endearments and their griefs, the learning of Abelard and the piety of Eloise, and English readers will find their memory embalmed in Alexander Pope's epistle from Eloise, as passionate and pathetic as any that Ovid ever wrote for his imaginary heroines.

There is a tomb similarly honored at Scutari. It is of the beautiful Fatima, the wife of a great and wealthy follower of Mohammed, who died in the sixteenth century. He was a warrior, as Abelard had been a monk; both, indeed, had fought; the one with the cimeter and the lance, the other with the weapons of the fiercest and sharpest polemics.

The dead of Spring Grove, sleep under a landscape of equal beauty with either of these. Their names are not so world-wide as those of Eloise and Fatima, but they, too, have fought their fight. There are among them the bones of soldiers who fell for their country, and the

dust of the leaders in the mighty army of those
who have led the vanguard of peaceful progress. The broad and beautiful avenue, with
its magnificent trees, brings the living and the
dead alike to the final abode of rest and release
from strife and contention, where there are
laurels and roses for the blue, lilies and myrtles
for the gray. After generations have passed
away, the massy granite, embedded in green
turf, shaded by trees then venerable with age,
and embosomed in flowers, may look down upon the graves of many whose lives have been
as romantic, if not so sad, as Eloise's---as deeply
loved as Fatima's. Then some poet, like
Pope, or some noble romancer like Scott, will
arise, and in another Epistle, or another ' Old
Mortality,' tell the tale of those who are gone."

THE AQUEDUCT.

Rome had fourteen aqueducts—Carthage has
but one. They cost the Empire millions of dollars—this, Carthage nothing. They brought
water to Rome—this conveys it to Carthage.
They had a " substruction of solid masonery "
—this of wood. They had no cascade or minne-
haha—this has. They were built upon the old
Latin principle in hydrostatics :
  " *Subit alitudinem exortus sui.*"—

so is this. *Aqua Nova*, one of the most magnificent, was 59 miles long and 109 feet high—this
is 200 feet long and 20 high. Roman architecture had some of its noblest exemplifications
in the construction and endowment of her
ancient artificial rivers—this is a simple specimen of modern wood work. They long since
yielded " to the tooth of time and razure of
oblivion "—this remains.

CHAPTER XII.

THE HAMILTON COUNTY FAIR GROUNDS.

WITHIN the last three years, about $25,000 have been expended in enlarging and improving these grounds. Forty-two acres are now within the enclosures.

Forty years ago, William Henry Harrison —for thirty days President of the United States —was the first President of this society. From that time down to the present, with few exceptions, have been held these feasts of the Wheat harvest, and First fruits and the Ingatherings—these autumnal convocations where men joyfully and gratefully commingle to compare as to how the earth has yielded her increase in response to the demands of the husbandman ; as to the improved methods of its culture by which labor is lightened and dignified and the more amply rewarded.

Within a hundred yards of this locality,* it is

---

* White's Station.

definitely known that a battle was fought with Indians for the control of this grand valley. Then the question was finally settled whether the tall, dark forests were to remain the home of the savage, or be felled by the axe of the frontiersman, in order that the rich unsunned soil might be opened to the sunshine and furrowed by the ploughman.

The wave set in motion by an Infinite hand for an infinite purpose rolled on, while upon its crest sat civilization sanctified by christianity. It waved a magical wand, and a wilderness became an Eden. The waste of woods, within three generations, has become a populous and powerful realm. And this is its highest evidence. It is an unspoken eulogy in praise of human progress. It is an unsung anthem, giving nature's God the glory for painting the rainbow upon the clouds, and saying : "While the earth remaineth, seedtime and harvest, and cold and heat, and summer and winter, and day and night, shall not cease."

That this institution stands so high to-day in popular esteem, is in the main attributable —aided by the intelligent and hearty co-operation of the Board of Directors—to the energy and executive ability and personal popularity fo its president, Col. W. H. Hill, of Sharon.

A LAND MARK

Is the old Sturgis homestead on Wayne
avenue in Maplewood. Generations have come
and gone since it was built. From its commanding site it has looked, approaching a
century, towards the East, recalling the stead-
fast gaze of the Egytian Sphynx through the
blinding sands of the desert and the sunshine and storms of passing ages. It has witnessed the flowing tide of population working
its channel up the valley from the great civic-
centre on the Ohio. It has seen the old
Hamilton road widen into a thoroughfare;
seen two iron highways constructed to the east
and west. When its walls were reared, it was
comparatively alone in its rural splendor.
The farm upon which it stood, with its orchard
and meadows and woodlands, spread away in
every direction from it. It has looked unen-
viously upon the beautiful houses that have
sprung up around it, as if children, who have
clothed themselves with finer architectural
raiment, in mild disregard, but with no dis-
dain for her old fashioned habiliments.

In point of durability it completely symbolizes the true idea of a home. No "contract
gothic sham" is this. Its superstructure was

reared in the hope and with the design that it should be an enduring earthly home, as well for him who planned and built it in the love of wife and children, as for all who should come after him, whether consanguineous or strangers to the ancestral blood.

Soon upon these old walls will be built a mansard roof and a tower, while within they are being decorated with Marston's choicest styles of Anglo-Japanese papers, as if it were to be a human habitation for generations to come.

This property was originally the home of the parents of Mrs. Joseph F. Mills; but now is owned and occupied by Mr. James S. Zerbe, Editor of the *American Inventor*.

AN OPERA HOUSE,

Centrally located in the suburb of Maplewood, at one time called Pille's but now known as " Mill's Opera house, is hardly of that style of architecture designated as the "Oriental Romanesque," but because of its severe simplicity it may be said to suggest that "chaste elegance peculiar to Italian architecture."

It is unlike the Pantheon; that was circular in form, this, rectangular. That consisted of

a " Rotunda, with a noble corinthian octa-
style portico attached to it," this does not.
That was approached by seven steps which
elevated it above the level of ancient Rome ;
this, but by two. The Pantheon was dedicated
to the worship of all the gods ; this, for a
while, was set apart for the worship of the only
true God. The splendor of the one has departed, that of this remains.

It is unlike the Coliseum. That was projected by the Emperor Vespasian ; this, by the
Emperor Joseph. That was built 1,900 years
ago ; this, within the last decade. That was an
ellipse, this, a parallelogram. Gaudentis was
the architect of that ; Mace of this. Gaudentis suffered martyrdom for his christian belief
within the very theatre he had planned ; the
architect of this still builds. The one reverbe-
rated to the groan of the dying Gladiator ;
this to " The Lay of the Last Minstrels."

It is unlike the Athenæum. There only poets,
philosophers and literary men met in the dis-
cussion of literary subjects. But this is not
exclusively an intellectual arena, although

" We, we have seen the intellectual giants stand,
Like Titans, face to face, Athos and Ida,
With a dashing sea of eloquence between."

But it is like the old FORUM ROMANUM in that
the length of it exceedeth the breadth by one-
third ; and in that here, too, justice is admin-
istered ; here, too, fair women and brave men
have commingled in the convivial assembly

" To sweeten talk and heel the high lavolt."

Here, too, the Village Amphictyonic Council
statedly convenes to deliberate upon municipal
affairs.

It is unlike Springer Music Hall. That is
dedicated to Minerva, the goddess of Art and
Industry ; this, rather, to Orpheus as having
" established social relations and inaugurated
civilization." That resounded to the music
of the Thomas Orchestra ; this, to the resonant
instruments of the Village Band. That
vibrated to the songs of Gerster and Valleria ;
this, to the voice of a *Carcy*. That is the civic
arena of inter-state art expositions ; this, of
church fairs and festivals.

Finally, a comparison is justifiable between
it and the old Athenian Academy—it being at
present used as a department preparatory to
entrance to the Public Schools.

" From that best academe
A mother's knee"

to this, and the first step is taken up the hill of Science.

Through all these changes and vicissitudes, like the old Flavian Amphitheatre, it remains —

" Simple, erect, severe, austere, sublime, —
Shrine of all saints and temple of all gods,
From Jove to Jesus."

CHAPTER. XIII.

THE BOGEN HOMESTEAD.

H AS for its eastern boundery the western corporate line of Hartwell, along which it extends about 1,000 feet, and thence sweeps upward and westward until it embraces about 275 acres, and constitutes what is known as "Hartwell Heights." Its contour is diversified with meadow, brook, rolling and wooded tracts, orchards and vineyards. The mansion is back three-quarters of a mile from Glendale avenue, and is approached by a beautiful drive, lined with 260 fruit-trees, whose branches almost touch over head.

The house is a wonderful old home. It is built of stone, dug from the adjoining hill side. Its cellar is thirty feet deep and 160 feet long.

While in this darksome place methought the castle walls of Chillon must be overhead and that another Bonnivard was chained to a "column stone" as its desolate prisoner. And yet we mused the while,—

"Chillon thy prison is a holy place,
  And thy sad floor an altar—for 'twas trod
Until his very steps have left a trace
  Worn, as if thy cold pavement were a sod,
By Bonnivard:—May none those marks efface!
  For they appeal from tyranny to God."

Above this subterranean vault rises the stony superstructure into massive proportions, resembling a castle in spaciousness within and solidity without.

One summer night we visited that home and looked upon the pictured walls and heard music and happy voices. And when the evening had closed it was to go away from a bright place and count as passed one more " green and sunny glade " in the journey of life at the old fashioned hospitable homestead of MR. AND MRS. GEORGE BOGEN.

MAJOR G. W. CORMANY'S PLACE.

The traveler, in passing along Glendale avenue or over the C. H. & D. railroad never fails to observe this attractive residence and its grounds. It has an exclusive location, being in the north-east corner of Rensselaer Park, fronting 304 feet on the pike and extending back to a line enclosing 7½ acres of ground.

The handsome residence of Doctor Bunker is just across the corporation line, and the depot is within two squares. This splendid property is on the western margin of the village of Hartwell, hanging there as an ornament upon her outskirts, near enough to be benefited by the municipal rule that regulates the affairs of the village and far enough to justify the plea of *quo warranto* should the city fathers seek to impose a tax as *quid pro quo*. You enter this villa through a gate that has always been admired for its symmetrical proportions. The avenue up to the house is wide and smooth and hard, sweeping around the house in a graceful curve. The ground set apart for lawn and shrubbery are highly ornamented, and kept in perfect order. The house is a two story frame, and, with the improvements completed, already designed, will command admiration, with its porches, mansard roof and tower. The stable is large, commodious and proportionate. The little farm then extends westward through which a pretty rivulet passes, singing—

> " I come from haunts of coot and hern
>   I make a sudden sally,
>   And sparkle out among the fern
>   To bicker down a valley."

In the green pasture beside that running brook may be seen at times the favorite family horse and the "lowing herd;" the ruminant goat and web-footed water-fowl of the order *anseres* including the palatable canvass-back; the clarion voiced peacock and omnivorous swine, so fat, that like Falstaff, they "lard the lean earth as they walk along." Around and over all the faithful dog keeps watch; meanwhile, "the harmless, necessary cat" is asleep in the sunshine.

This home, together with all the rights, privileges and appurtenances thereunto appertaining and belonging, corporeal and incorporeal, was the objective point of a marital campaign entered upon in the year 1867 by MAJOR AND MRS. GEORGE W. CORMANY.

THE W. R. MORRIS HOMESTEAD.

We have read somewhere of somebody's ancestral home built upon a cliff that frowned

"O'er old Conway's foaming flood;"

And this passage, floating in the mind since childhood, was recalled to memory by a visit to this venerable mansion, built forty years ago

by the departed father of William R. Morris,
Esq., the present owner.

This house is on an acclivitous bluff at whose
base Mill creek at times foams and roars like
a furious flood, resembling

> " The tumbling surf, that buries
>   The Orkneyan skerries
> Answering the hoarse Hebrides."

This old fashioned homestead is one of
the most interesting and beautiful of the many
noble places in this valley.   It is interesting
because of historical reminiscences.   It was
doubtless selected as a place of residence because of the natural beauty of its site and surroundings.   Storm after storm has over-swept it.
It lifts its walls but one story high at the front, but
its foundations are broad and deep and its am-
plified rooms compensate for the want of ad-
ditional stories.   The farm upon which it
stands, once belonged to old Captain Jacob
White.   White's station was at the foot of this
hill distant not more than one thousand feet.
The Indians haunted this lovely spot.   From it
they made the assault on the little stockade,
and when repulsed retreated over the same
spot.   The big Indian chief, killed while in the
act of scaling the fort, was buried at last in a

corner of the lot where the house now stands. His long bones, enormous skull, and glistening teeth still imbedded in the massive jaws, his battle axe and some trinkets were afterwards exhumed when the lot was being graded.

The present owner might have been seen with that grinning skull in his hands musing like another Hamlet:

"Here's fine revolution, and we had the trick to see it! That skull had a tongue in it and could sing once. Why does he suffer this rude knave now to knock him about the sconce with a dirty shovel? Where be your gibes now, your gambol, your songs, your flashes of merriment that were wont to set the camp in a roar? not one now to mock your own grinning?"

And then thinking perhaps it might be a case of mistaken identity, and that it possibly was a " Pliocene skull," he addressed it thus, in the words of Francis Bret Harte.

> "Fragmentary fossil!
> Primal pioneer of pliocene formation,
> Hid in lowest drifts below the earliest stratum
>   Of volcanic tufa!
> Tell us of that scene—the dim and watery woodland,
> Songless, silent, stirless, with never bird or insect,
> Veiled with spreading fronds and screened with tall
>   club-mosses."

THE STROBEL HOMESTEAD.

Belonging to Mrs. L. A. Strobel, the wife of the professional musician, J. W. Strobel, Esq., is situated upon what is known as East Hartwell Heights, and about one-half of a mile distant from the Short Line depot. This is a musician's home. Orpheus has a profound devotee in "the lord of this manor." The site of the home, and the home itself, bespeak this. We heard the sound of stringed instruments within those walls one mild September evening. They recalled the old story of the elder Orpheus which inspired Miss Emma Cranch to sing so acceptably in one of our musical festivals

"I have lost my Eurydice,
 Nothing equals now my grief,
Hope, nor maddening unbelief,
 Nothing comes to my relief."

May we repeat a little of the strange and classic story? How that Orpheus had for his wife a nymph named Eurydice, who died from the bite of a serpent as she was flying from Aristæus, and that, disconsolate at her loss, he determined to descend to the lower world, to endeavor to mollify its rulers, and obtain permission for his beloved Eurydice to return to the region of light. Armed only with his lyre, he entered the realms of Hades, and gained an easy admittance to the Palace of Plato. At the music of his " golden shell," to borrow the beautiful language of ancient poetry, the wheel of Ixion stopped, Tantalus forgot the thirst that tormented him, the vulture ceased to prey on the vitals of Tityos, and Plato and Proserpina lent a favoring ear to his prayer. Eurydice was allowed to return with him to the upper world, but only on condition that Orpheus should not look back upon her before they had reached the confines of the kingdom of darkness. He broke the condition and she vanished out of his sight. At his death Jupiter placed his lyre in the skies.

THE CARLISLE VILLA.

There is a lonely eminence in western Wyoming dimly seen from the valley through the summer foliage, but plainly visible when "leaves have their time to fall." Somewhat alienated from its neighboring hill tops, it reminds you of "Jura in her misty shroud" when the eye seeks it through the blue veil

with which nature sometimes obscures from
view the rough outlines of her mountain chains.
Let us seek that summit from the standpoint
of the valley. You will realize that after all it
will not be as hazardous an enterprise as scaling the Matterhorn or any of the lesser Alps.
To do so we take a popular pleasure drive up
Glendale avenue, through the heart of Wyoming, to Reily avenue, then westwardly up that
ascending road to the Park Picturesque Villa
of MR. AND MRS. JOHN CARLISLE. It stands
amid old trees whose mission is as well to shield
from sunshine as guard from storms its rock-
built, palatial walls. In contemplating this
magnificent rural retreat, you realize what a
beautiful thought of a home is here embodied.
Nature has lavished her charms upon the site,
first lifting it to this commanding altitude and
then robing it with splendors from an infinite
source. The hand of affluence then erected this
superstructure of such surpassing loveliness.

Gracefully grotesque in out line ; surprising
you at all points with its departures from the
methodical house architecture of the day, it
seems a conglomerate of different styles, the
fittest of all surviving in this. The architect
must have been a law unto himself, *Sui gener's*,
or it stands a real home built from an ideal
formed from traveling in many lands.

The ground, sloping to the southward de-clivitously, forms an immense ravine, suggests Coleridge's description of Kubla Kahn's pleas-ure grounds:

> " But, oh ! that deep romantic chasm which slanted
> Down the green hill athwart a cedarn cover :
> A savage place! as holy and enchanted
> As e're beneath a waning moon was haunted
> By woman wailing for her demon lover."

MR. GEO. S. STEARN'S RESIDENCE.

It is said of Kenilworth castle, that the stately structure itself, which rose near the centre of a spacious enclosure, was composed of a huge pile of magnificent castellated buildings. The external wall of this royal castle was adorned and defended on the south and west sides by a lake partly artificial. " We cannot but add " —says Sir Walter Scott—" that this lovely palace, where princes feasted and heroes fought, now in the bloody earnest of storm and siege, and now in the games of chivalry, where beauty dealt the prize, which valor won, all is now desolate. The bed of the lake is now a rushy swamp; and the massive ruins of the castle only serve to show what their splendor once was, and to impress on the musing

visitor the transitory value of human posses-
sions, and the happiness of those who enjoy a
humble lot in virtuous contentment." It was
the royal home of Robert Dudley and Amy
Robsart as the Earl and Countess of Leicester,
and yet a most miserable home; for its very
magnificence gave origin doubtless to the favor-
itism of Elizabeth for the Earl; to his consequent estrangement from Amy, and her final
banishment to Cumnor Hall, that the queen
might be kept in ignorance of the fact that
Leicester had ever loved another than his sov-
ereign when she came to make that celebrated
visit to Dudley's Castle.

One morning, all alone, a gentleman took a
walk through unincorporated Wyoming. His
pathway lay westward along the dividing line
between the Friend and Woodruff homesteads.
He found himself at length upon an eminence. A field of ripening corn was round and
about him. But the long green blades, the
tall stalks, like nodding plumes, the tasseled
ears, he heeded not. He came not there to
pluck the ears of corn. He looked around and
away to the Reading hills whence he had
come. He saw that it was a beautiful site. A
thought of home was in his heart, and it must
be unbosomed—it must be embodied. And
so he said: Here will I found and build.

That pathway is now a sweeping avenue; and that thought found embodiment in the stately home of Mr. and Mrs. George S. Stearns. We never look upon its walls and tower, its spacious grounds and lake, without thinking them typical at least, of the past splendors of that old ruined historic castle; and yet so dissimilar, especially in that it is a happy as well as magnificent home, and in that *Amy*, though absent, was not banished from this modern Kenilworth.

MR. ELISHA P. STOUT'S

Splendid country seat in Wyoming, consisting of twenty-eight acres culminating in an eminence as commanding as that upon which stands the Carlisle Villa immediately to the South, claims our attention because of its extraordinary merits as a monument to the wonderful growth of this valley, and because of historical reminiscences suggested by the name of him who first built it. REILY is a noted name in western annals.

In 1792, John Reily settled upon a tract of land adjoining White's station on the south, from which he was driven by the Indians, and thereupon returned to Columbia, and resumed his occupation of school teaching. But in after years, his son, Col. Robert Reily, returned to the pioneer home of his father, looked around this beautiful country, selected this spot and built thereon a stone mansion and proceeded to beautify and adorn it. When the Rebellion broke out, he joined the army in defense of that home and his country, and was killed at the battle of Chancellorsville, being Colonel of the 75th Ohio Infantry at the time.

The title subsequently passed through Geo. D. Winchell, Esq., to the present owner, who, by lavish expenditure and cultivated taste, has greatly enlarged and embellished it. Nature has no resources or reserves of shrubbery which have not been laid under contribution to adorn it.

All kinds of plants grow there. Vines cling to the walls of old gray stone, aspiring to climb the steep slate roof and the towers that point upward through the branches of the trees that stand in majesty around it. The trees! how many secrets their tongues will never tell, but leave us as we stand beneath them to dream or conjecture as to what they have seen transpire under their branches!

We claim them as familiar friends. We love and caress them. We lean as lovers against

their strong, storm-defying trunks. They in
return yield us shade, and fruit, and flowers.
They cast their leafy crowns at our feet; they
bow their tall heads at the stroke of the axe
and become fuel for the hearth-stone;—but
their history their tongues will never tell.
They have done as much in response to the
caress of the Indian maiden of old as to the
pale face damsel of to-day; as much for the
Savage, who, doubtless, has glared down
upon White's station that sheltered the elder
Reily, as for the heoric son who broke this
woodland silence with the sound of the ham-
mer in erecting this mansion, and then laid
him down and died the patriot's death.

So we will leave the mysterious realm of the
trees to the tuneful birds, the viewless winds,
and the intercepted sunshine, and for a
moment, enter this rock-built house that
seems as enduring as the ancient hill it
crowns. Crossing the Mosaic threshold, the
massive doors opening on their bronzed hinges
in a welcoming way, you enter a hall that
connects with a labyrinth of rooms. All that
taste can devise and wealth provide cover the
floors and walls. You need go no further to
be impressed with the truth that this is one of
the homes characterized by Wendell Phillips as
" the consummate flower of our civilization.'

You recall at once the "Antique Oratory" of the old hall at Annesley, where a gifted poet met and loved a "rare and radiant maiden," but because his impassioned love was unrequited,

> "He passed from out the massive gates of that old hall,
> And mounting on his steed he went away,
> And ne'er repassed that hoary threshold more."—

And but for which the intellectual world would never have read "Childe Harold's Pilgrimage."

WAYNE AVENUE, M. E. CHURCH

Stands on the west side of Wayne avenue in Lockland. Together with the parsonage, it cost over $40,000, and was built within the past five years. The munificent donations of Col. * C. W. Friend, Thomas Fox, Esq., Gideon G. Palmer, Esq., George House, Esq., and others, made it possible for this congregation to build and dedicate to God—free from debt—this, the most beautiful and costly church in the valley, of which, at present, the Rev. Adam Bowers is pastor.

---

* Col. Friend was President of the Board of Trustees at the time of his death, which occurred shortly after the

That there is at work in society a *spiritual* civilization it will scarcely be denied.

Look at the churches and the school houses of this valley! They have kept pace with the march of emigration, and thus illustrate the truthful sentiment that " There has ever been a motion, a gravitation, more or less palpable, towards a man who should be the complement of every other man—the perfectness of manhood embodied in Jesus Christ."

The Poet, in imagination, standing perhaps on this very spot ninety years ago said :

> " I hear the tread of pioneers,
> Of nations yet to be,
> The first low wash of waves where soon
> Shall roll a human sea."

We are realizing this dream, and as the wave of Christian civilization swept over these

---

dedication in June, 1880. One of his last official acts was to present this church, in behalf of his congregation, through the Bishop, to Almighty God, saying, in the words of Solomon:

"I have surely built thee a house to dwell in, a setted place to abide in forever."

His life's work seemed then finished—and as one of the Pioneers of this valley and Methodism, he was gathered to his fathers. How many precious stones—onyx, chalcedony and amethyst—his liberal hands laid in those shining walls!

hills and valleys, it left no higher or better evidence of its divine origin and mission than this church.

We look with sadness upon the old churches falling into disuse and decay, or perhaps subserving other ends, but the heart takes hope and faith is intensified when we realize that larger and grander edifices have taken their places.

This sacred dwelling is but the outgrowth of one of those old structures. And so it has always been. The movable tabernacle in the wilderness finally became the magnificent temple of Solomon, but not until the Salem of Melchisedec became the Jerusalem of King David.

From its belfry you can tell all the towers of this valley and see almost its entire extent.

Its tall spire points as well to the poor as the rich man's heaven.   And its bell

> " How it swells,
>   How it dwells
> On the future ; how it tells
> Of the rapture that impels
> To the swinging and the ringing
>   Of the bells, bells, bells,
>   What a world of happiness
> Its harmony foretells."

CHAPTER XIV.

LUDLOW'S STATION.

ISRAEL LUDLOW came from Morris-
town, New Jersey, to the North-west Territory, soon after the passage of the ordinance of
1787. He came, expecting to assist in surveying and establishing the bounderies of the
Miami purchase. In the early part of the year
1789 he became associated with Mathiar Denman and Robert Patterson, in the proprietor-
ship and founding of Cincinnati.

On the 9th day of March, 1790, he entered
land warrants, Nos. 83 and 84, and located the
west half of section 22, T. 3, F. R. 2, M. P.,
which is now a part of Cumminsville, and soon
afterwards established a station there. Among
those who formed the settlement were James
Miller, Joseph and Enoch McHendry, Daniel
Bates, Uriah Hardesty, Frederick Patchel,
John Noble Cummins, Jonathan Pierson, Enos
Terry, and Thomas Goudy.† Some time dur-

---

† From Olden's Sketches :—Thomas Goudy was a native of

ing the same year they erected a block-house,
where Knowlton street intersects the Cincinnati, Hamilton and Dayton Railroad, and a
little south of the Christian church. A Mr.
Abner Boston had a cabin near the station,
where he and his family lived for a number of
years.

This station is noted as being the place
where General St. Clair organized his army.
He moved his command from Fort Washington
on the 7th day of August, 1791, and encamped
at Ludlow station, where he remained until the
17th day of September following, when he took
up his march for the Indian villages. After
his defeat, and while the remnant of his forces
were returning to Fort Washington, they again
encamped at this station. On arriving there
they found the settlement entirely deserted, not
a settler remained. The soldiers found shelter
in the cabins and block-house over night, and
next morning, in a forlorn condition, moved
down to Fort Washington.

The station was soon afterwards re-occupied

Pennsylvania, a lawyer by profession. He came to Cincinnati as early as, 1789, and was, it is said, the first lawyer in
the town. In 1793 he married Sarah Wallace, sister of John
S. Wallace. He was the father of Mrs. Sarah Clark, who is
still living with her sons, Alexander C. Clark, north of Reading, in Sycamore Township.

by a few families, among whom was Abner Boston.*

It does not appear that Mr. Ludlow resided at the station until after peace was established with the Indians in 1795. His interest and his business were at Cincinnati, and there he lived until after the treaty of Greenville, when he built a dwelling house some distance north of the block-house, which he made his permanent residence. A portion of this building is said to be still standing, and is erroneously called the "station house."

THE LUDLOW MANSION.

This ancestral home, older than the nineteenth century and ivy-mantled with historic associations, claims more than a passing notice.

The history of the Miami Country—of Hamilton County—especially of Mill Creek valley, is in part the history of this venerable structure. Once it stood in the centre of an almost impenetrable forest; now, the sounds of a teeming population are heard on every hand and myriads

---

* Boston was a native of Virginia, and married the widow of William Risk, her maiden name was Margaret Wilkinson. James Risk, now of Cumminsville, is the grandson of Mrs. Boston.

of less distinguished but more beautiful homes, from the palatial residences on Clifton heights, to the pretty cottages of Cumminsville, look down upon and environ it. Once a large lawn, shadowed by tall trees, swept down to the banks of Mill creek upon which children played who are now our pioneers, if peradventure they have not fallen into "the deep tranquillity of endless sleep." The human wave that brought its founders here from the east has swept onward until it has reached and populated the golden shores of the distant Pacific. Willows, a century old, wave wierd branches over the self same spring that slaked the thirst of the Indian first and then his pale faced foe.

The writer once visited this relic of the past. Passing across the low-roofed porch he entered the folding doors at the touch of the old fashioned latch, into a room-like vestibule. Antique, angular stairs lead up to the second story —then to the attic. This stair-way by reason of associations, may well be compared to that in the Probasco Palace, although the latter stair-way it is asserted, cost $25,000.

Upon entering, we were met and warmly welcomed by MR. ISAAC B. MCFARLAND, a venerable pioneer—who, with his family, is at present in charge of the property. He seemed

to have " come down from former generations"
as he familiarly talked of those who had
lived therein—and of our distinguished and
departed fore-fathers whose names are so
brightly and indissolubly linked with our past.
Four score years have passed over his white-
ened head—yet with unclouded mind and
memory, and with much warmth of heart, he
walked the path of life backward to childhood.
Hearing him, the writer had but little need to
ask,
                    —" How is it
        That this lives in thy mind? What seest thou else
        In the dark backward and abysm of time ?

Had he done so Miranda's answer to Prospero would have followed :

                    —" 'Tis far off,
        And rather like a dream than an assurance,
        That my remembrance warrants."

This property now belongs to Mrs. CATHARINE
LUDLOW WHITEMAN, a direct descendant of
Colonel Israel Ludlow, who built it about the
year 1795—or shortly after the Greenville
treaty which secured the valley from Indian
depredations.   It was at first a log structure
subsequently covered with weather boarding.
At the time of its completion it was the best

looking and largest house in Cincinnati or its
vicinity, says the late Dr. E. D. Mansfield in
his "Personal memories."

*Col. Jared Mansfield, professor of Natural
and Experimental Philosophy in the United
States Military Academy, lived in this house
from 1805 to 1809—part of it being used as his
office while engaged in surveying the Miami
Purchase. It stands on a bluff made by the
C. H. & D. Railroad when constructed immediately to the east of it, and can be distinctly
seen from the cars, its particular locality being
a short distance north of the present station in
Cumminsville. A few venerable evergreens
seem to stand as monuments around it. Twelve
years ago an addition was made to the southern end of the house—adding much to its appearance. The oldest portion is the northern.

Within, its old fashioned walls are papered
after the latest styles—its old fashioned fire
place is now filled in with a modern grate—its
old fashioned mantels somewhat relieved of
their austerity by bric-a-brac—its low ceilings
seemingly heigthened by rich wall paper.

In and out of that old portal have passed,
Col. Israel Ludlow,   John Cleves Symmes,
Col. Jared Mansfield,   Gen. Arthur St. Clair,

* This was the father of Hon. E. D. Mansfield.

Gen. Anthony Wayne, Gov. Return J. Meigs,
Little Turtle, Bok-on-ja-ha-lus,
Gen. Wm. H. Harrison, Gov. E. A. Brown,
Gov. T. Worthington, Hon. Lewis Cass,
Hon. Salmon P. Chase, Gen. J. C. Totten,
Hon. Judge Burnet. Gen. Gano,
Nicholas Longworth, Judge D. K. Este,
Oliver M. Spencer, Gen. William Lytle,
Judge Goforth, Gen. J. H. Piatt.
Mrs. Charlotte Chambers Ludlow,
and many other distinguished men and women
whose names add lustre to the history of Cin-
cinnati.

It is an illustrious land mark. Looking upon
these remnants of its past splendor and moved
by the " still rhetoric " of the associations that
haunt it, the words of Byron, when musing
among the ruins of Rome, come to you—

> " Tully was not so eloquent as thou,
> Thou nameless column with the buried base !
> What are the laurels of the Caesar's brow?
> Crown me with ivy from his dwelling place ?

BOK-ON-JA-HA-LUS,

Was chief of the Delaware Indians. He was
deemed almost a civilized man, because of his
having been much under the influence of the

Moravian missionaries. He was highly en-
dowed with mental strength, and it is said of
him that no Christian knight was ever more
scrupulous in performing his treaty engage-
ments.

He was a natural hero, possessing great dig-
nity of character.

St. Clair owed his defeat to the presence of
such chieftains as Little Turtle, Bok-on-ja-ha-
lus, and Blue Jacket, chief of the Shawanese.

The following incident, related of this celebrated warrior, occurred immediately after the
battle of Fallen Timbers. Our victorious army,
in pursuit of the Indians, finally halted and
encamped for three days upon the banks of the
Maumee, within sight of the British fort, which
had afforded protection and encouragement to
the Indians :—

General Wayne had received private instruc-
tions from President Washington that, should
he find himself in sufficient force to capture the
British fort, he was to do so, and drive the garrison out of the country. He accordingly carefully inspected the works. They had an arm-
ament of ten pieces of artillery, and were gar-
risoned by four hundred and fifty men. It was
therefore decided that the attempt to storm the
fort would result in great slaughter, and probably in a failure.

After the defeat, the officers of the fort did not venture to open its gates to receive the fugitive savages. This would have been, indeed, a declaration of war against the United States. As the British had encouraged the Indians, in every possible way before the battle, they were greatly disgusted by this unexpected treatment. One of their celebrated chiefs— Bok-on-ja-ha-lus, of whom we are writing and who had fled down the river, beyond the fort, assembled his tribe in a little fleet of canoes, to ascend the stream and enter into a treaty of peace with the victors. As they were approaching the fort, the officer of the day hailed Bok-on-ja-ha-lus, and said that Major Campbell wished to speak to him.

*"In that case," said the proud chieftain, "let him come to me."

"That will never do," was the reply; "and he will not allow you to pass the fort unless you comply with his wishes."

"What shall prevent my passing?" the chief responded.

"Those guns," answered the orderly, as he pointed to the artillery which could sweep the stream with grapeshot.

---

* From Abbot's History of Ohio.

"I fear not your cannon," the chief replied. "After suffering the Americans to insult your flag, without daring to fire upon them, you must not expect to frighten Bok-on-ja-ha-lus.'"

The canoes pushed on, and passed the fort unmolested.

Mrs. Charlotte Chambers Ludlow — the gifted, accomplished and christian wife of Col. Israel Ludlow—in a letter to Rev. Dr. Boudinot, dated at Ludlow station, gives this interesting account of a visit she received from Bok-on-ja-ha-lus and his friend Kin-ka-boxkie, at that place :

"About the year 1800, in the month of June, near the middle of the day, as I sat in my parlor at Ludlow station, commanding a view of the smooth green yard, slightly shaded from the fervor of the sun by the depending boughs of three luxuriant willows, which a few years had brought to sentimental perfection—with feelings in perfect accordance with the harmony of the scene, I experienced a tranquillity of mind to which I had been for some time a stranger, and forgot for the moment that there was in all the world a human being less happy than myself.

I was interrupted by the entrance of two strangers of uncommon interest. The first was

my old friend, the Delaware chief, Bok-on-ja-
ha-lus. I rose to meet him with a cordial
welcome. After taking my hand, he said,
"La-na-pak-wa (a name given me by the
Delaware Indians) this is my friend Kin-ka-
box-kie." They took their seats, and informed
me that they had called for the purpose of taking dinner, having made the engagement with
my husband in town. They were on their return from seeing the Great Father, as they
called the President.

At dinner they received my attentions as persons of good breeding in those circles where
good breeding excludes every useless ceremony.
Kin-ka-box-kie was taciturn. When he
spoke, it was in the Delaware tongue. He de-
sired his friend to tell me that he could not
speak English. Bok-on-ja-ha-lus informed me
that the President had said "they must improve their lands; their young men must learn
to plough; their young women must learn to
spin." He seemed dejected, but he was noble
in his deportment. While we sat conversing
at the table after the cloth was removed, he
said, "Lah-na-pak-wa, we now go." "And
when shall I see you again, Bok-on-ja-ha-lus?"
said I. "Me old; me soon lay down," said he,
with a horizontal motion of his hand. Then

raising his eyes to Heaven, with an ardent emotion, he added with an effusion of feeling I have never seen more expressive, " But we shall meet with Jesus." I took his hand, inquiring with rapture, " Bok-on-ja-ha-lus do you know Jesus?" He answered with firmness, " Me know Jesus; me love Jesus." Then rising from the table, they shook hands with me, solemnly saying farewell. My eyes followed their venerable figures until the door closed from my view for the last time in this world Bok-on-ja-ha-lus and his friend."

PARTING WORDS.

—" Farewell! a word which hath been
And must be,—a sound which makes us linger,
Yet, farewell"!

The following touching farewell to Ludlow station and to Mill creek is from the same gifted pen :

September 1, 1820.

" Accompanied by my dear friend Mrs. Mc-Farland,† and my two little daughters, I made a farewell visit to Ludlow station   *   * After repose, we rambled over the woodland.

---

† Mrs. Stephen McFarland, the mother of Isaac B. McFarland, Esq., now occupying the Ludlow Mansion.

Softly murmuring flowed the beloved stream of
Mill creek. Precious to my view are its ver-
dure-clad banks. Often with the husband of
my youth have I climbed the hills around ; often,
seated in the cool shade, has he narrated the
dangers of early times, while yet the savage
foot-prints were fresh in its sand."

G. A. R.

The surviving soldiers of the union army,
living upon this classic ground, having organized themselves as a band of brothers under
the name signified by the above initials, and
remembering their comrade of illustrious line
age, and his bright record as a soldier, call
themselves, "ISRAEL LUDLOW, Post No. 76,
Grand Army of the Republic."

November the 7, 1881, an event took place
at the Post which should be mentioned in this
connection, as bearing upon the history of the
Ludlows ;—it was the presentation of a Bible
and a Flag, by Mrs. C. L. Whiteman and Mr.
Dunlap Ludlow, of Illinois ; Mrs. Hunt, of New
Orleans ; and General Ben. Ludlow, of Texas.

Chaplain J. F. Myers made the presentation.
speec hin behalf of the relatives, in the following
befitting words :—

"No more worthy or noble name could have been conferred upon our Post than his—a descendant of that old pioneer Israel Ludlow, who was appointed by Washington as a surveyer in the North-west Territory, who laid out the city of Cincinnati, and established a station in our own immediate vicinity for the refuge of the settler from the attack of Indians, and opened up the settlement of the Mill Creek valley, before Ohio became a State. His old home is still standing as a landmark of early times. This was the home of his grandson Israel Ludlow, a son worthy of his sire. When the war of 1861 broke out, he was among the first to go forth at the call of his country to assist in defending its honor and maintaining its integrity. He enlisted as a private in the Sixth Ohio Infantry, and afterward obtained an appointment as a Lieutenant in Terrill's Regular battery. He participated in the battles of Shiloh, Stone River and Chicamauga. In the latter he was severely wounded and taken prisoner by the enemy. At the close of the war he came home and practiced law, but the wound received and the privations endured had undermined his health, and at last, in 1873, he was taken off by disease, in the prime of early manhood. Thus did he give himself up as a sacri-

fice to his country, after having seen treason
subdued and peace restored."

CUMMINS *vs.* HUTCHINSON.

We are indebted to the facile pen of an educated gentleman,* now residing in Cumminsville, for the following information which we
give in his own language:

"In the triangle formed by the avenue, Hamilton pike, and Blue Rock street, about forty
years ago, was the extensive tannery of David
Cummins, after whom the town was named.
On the knoll above was the Hutchinson tavern, where now is Mr. Hoffner's residence.
A steady stream of pure water flowed then, as
now, from the bank below the house, and Mr.
Cummins, by his deed, was entitled to use as
much water from that spring for his tannery,
as would flow through "five three-quarter inch
auger holes." With the Hutchinson's tavern
was a farm of two hundred acres, and they
kept a dairy. One very dry summer, Mrs.
Hutchinson plugged up the holes of the tannery pipe so that her cows should not suffer.
The tanner's boys opened it; again it was
closed. High words succeeded and frequently

---

* Prof. M. S. Turrill—Principal of the Public Schools.

blows. Reports and threats were circulated by servant girls and others. Private injuries were inflicted, and personal animosities showed themselves in aggressions and bitter retaliations. Young orchards were girdled, horses hamstrung, and tanvats destroyed. Outrages became so frequent that the town then got the name generally given to the hottest known place. Then came the contests in court, lawsuits, trials, appeals, lawyer's fees, heavy costs, &c., &c. and both contestants, hitherto finely prospering, became poor. One mortgaged his farm to the United States Bank to raise the wherewithal to carry on his suit; the other borrowed from his friends, and as long as any money could be raised to pay charges the courts permitted the contest to continue.

The United States Bank, throught its agent, Mr. T. Kirby, took Mr. Hutchinson's farm for the money furnished by them, which amounted, with interest, to about $9,000. Mr. Hoffner purchased forty-seven acres of the choicest part, with the tavern included, for $5,000, and Mr. Kirby satisfied the rest of the debt by accepting a deed from the bank for the remaining one hundred and fifty acres, which was considered a splendid investment for him.

The tan yard fell into Mr. Knowlton's hands,

who has retained possession of it ever since,
and is nearly all covered with dwelling-houses
and stores.

Further along the avenue is the Dr. Mount
homestead, where he, as practicing physician,
resided for nearly forty years.
Beyond is the Ludlow Station farm, the old
mansion of which is still standing, also the old
"station house," the silk factory, erected in
Morris Multicaula's days, the spring that has
flowed unfailingly for eighty years, its waters
now gathered in a gravelly bowl, forming a
baptismal font for the Christian Church near
by, and also the site of General Wayne's army
encampment while on his way to humiliate the
Indians of North-western Ohio."

THE OLD CAMP GROUNDS.

Do we dream? Are things what they seem?
Is human life an ever widening, an ever deepening river, poured from an "exhaustless urn"
and rushing out of the voiceless past into the
viewless future? Do they only live who for the
moment are poised upon the crest of the foremost wave, and then sink to give place to those
who, crowding, follow? Our fathers, where are
they? and the prophets, do they live forever?

Or is humanity like a mighty pyramid, whose foundations were laid when the morning stars sang together, rising generation upon generation, age after age, until it shall meet the Son of Man in his coming, and, at the final consummation, be touched with a never ending glory?

Here, upon this old camping ground, we can look three generations down the sides of that pyramid, and in imagination see our forefathers toiling upon its foundations laid in patriotism and cemented with their blood. They built for us, therefore are we higher in point of privilege than they. Are we both preserving what they have transmitted, and building for those who shall come up after us?

Here, where we walk about—rows of human habitations prescribing our pathways — the smoke of factories filling our eyes—the rumble of vehicles, the roar of trains, the shrieks of the locomotive greeting and grating upon the ear— encamped first the decimated army under the stately St. Clair; and then the victorious one under the impetuous Wayne.

Here were heard and seen :

> " The neighing steed, and the shrill trump,
> The spirit-stirring drum, the ear-piercing fife,
> The royal banner."

A change! After the lapse of years, the old camping ground becomes a field for general muster, which recalls a sight vividly remembered by many now living :—

"Then the old fashioned Colonel
Galloped through the white infernal
Powder cloud;
And his broad sword was swinging
And his brazen throat was ringing
Trumpet loud."

Another change! Sumter is fired upon! the "tempest torrent and whirlwind" of patriotism over sweeping the land! Camp Gurley is the scene of an encampment! It becomes the camping ground of some of the descendants of the heroes of the revolution and the war of 1812. Some went from that now classic ground, who are among the "unreturning brave." Many returned and to-day are numbered among the best citizens of this community.

The writer first saw Cumminsville in 1861, as a member of the 4th Ohio Cavalry, and first saw in that encampment the one to whom these pages are affectionately dedicated. The reader will therefore pardon the insertion of this scrap of history. .

* INCIDENT AT CAMP GURLEY.

" The monotony of life at Camp Gurley was varied Saturday afternoon by the arrival of a party of ladies from Glendale, among whom were Mrs. Col. Stanley Matthews, Mrs. Judge Cilley, Mrs. Samuel J. Thompson, Mrs. R.W. Keyes, and brought with them an elegant dinner for Co. B. of the 4th Ohio Cavalry, Colonel John Kennet commanding. The men did ample justice to the delicacies set before them, after which three hearty cheers were given for the fair donors of the feast, and as many more for the glorious old flag that floated over them. Colonel Kennet and the field officers of the regiment were present at the entertainment. Short and appropriate speeches were made, and the band of the regiment discoursed some of its best music, giving zest to the occasion."

"We've been tenting to-day on the old
        Camp ground,
    Thinking of days gone by,
    Of the loved ones at home that gave us
        the hand,
    And the tear that said " Good bye ! ""

THE ST. PHILIP'S EPISCOPALIAN CHURCH.

This tasteful edifice is a remarkable instance

* From the Cincinnati Gazette, 1861.

illustrating the growth of church interests in our valley.

It stands upon a lot donated by the late Timothy Kirby, Esq.—the site commanding beautiful views in all directions. It cost $7,000, is entirely free from debt, and was consecrated 1874.

Mrs. Robert Bowler once looked from her baronial home it Clifton, and saw a field white for the harvest. And did the angels become the reapers? It would seem so, for it was not long afterward that Mrs. Bowler, Mrs. David James, Mrs. General H. B. Banning, and other christian ladies were engaged in mission work in Cumminsville, under the auspices of the Episcopal Church in Clifton. Services were first held in Dodsworth Hall, and then in the Christian Church. Then the "Church Guild" of Cincinnati fostered this spiritual enterprise. The first clergyman officiating was the Rev. E. P. Wright, Rector of St. James church of the city; then the Rev. Mr. Kellogg; then the Rev. Mr. Mortimer of "Grace Church" Clifton. At the consecration Rev. John H. Ely, became its first resident Rector, at which time it finally separated from the parent church of Clifton.

Many are drinking from that spiritual rock
smitten by gentle loving hands in the name of
the Redeemer of mankind.

Some have been translated from this mount
—not long since a distinguished Christian soldier's name was transcribed to the rolls of the
church not made with hands—GEN. HENRY B.
BANNING.

" In deeds of love excel ! excel !
Chimed out from ivied-towers a bell ;
    This is the church not built on sand,
Emblem of one not built with hands ;
Its forms and sacred rites revere,
Come worship here! Come worship here !
In rituals and faith excel !
Chimed out the Episcopalian bell ! "

THE PRESBYTERIAN CHURCH.

An old log school-house once stood about
where the Kirby homestead now stands.
Preaching first began there in 1832.—Rev.
David Fergus, of the Presbyterian church and
father of Mrs. Janet Langland officiating. The
Rev. David Root of College Hill occasionally
preached there.

In 1852 the present Presbyterian church edifice was projected, the lot being donated by Mrs.
Janet Langland, Mr. John Thompson and Mrs.

Janet Thompson. But it was not ready for services before November, 1854.

From a discourse delivered November 28, 1867, by Rev. A. J. Reynolds, then Pastor of the Cumminsville Presbyterian Church, many interesting facts may be obtained relative to rise and progress of the religious enterprises of this place. He casts up the spiritual account and there is much to the credit of these noble organizations for the good done to humanity.

The mortuary history of this church is touchingly epitomized in the following passage taken from a Historical Sketch written by Prof. M. S. Turrell.

"Our bell has tolled its funeral knell for many—for the babe with the smile of innocence resting upon its face in its last sleep,—for the youth whose life was so soon over,—for the young man just ready to enter upon 'the world's broad field of battle,'—for those of maturer years called away in the midst of their usefulness,—for now and then one who had lived life's allotted time—three score years and ten,—for members of our families, the young, the beautiful, the honored."

The Presbyterian Sabbath School began nearly as soon as the church building was finished. He says " during the war, the church and sabbath school were well represented in the army"—we may be permitted to add that one of those soldiers returned when the war ended, bearing honorable scars, and is now its superintendent, Henry N. Van Dyke.

EPHRAIM KNOWLTON.

Sixty years ago this venerable pioneer came to Cincinnati and but a year or two afterwards located his dwelling and store at the junction of the old Wayne road (now Spring Grove avenue, leading up through Carthage to Hamilton), and the old St. Clair road, finding its way to Hamilton by way of College Hill, and Mount Pleasant. This house was subsequently burned; he thereupon built the present stone structure now occupied as a store, and known as " Knowlton's Corner " as familiarly as " Fountain Square," to which likewise it is comparable in having a natural fountain of waters far more delicious as a beverage, though flowing through an old wooden pump, than that which pours continuously through bronzed tubes to supply Cincinnati with Ohio river water.

This well of water has been springing up for nearly sixty years—seemingly a source, and certainly an emblem, of everlasting life;—

as if its "swift half intermitted burst" were
forced from Alph, the sacred river, which
Coleridge portrays as running

> " Through caverns measureless to man
> Down to a sunless sea."

The time may come when here shall stand
a statue, in marble or in bronze, to be known
as " Knowlton's Fountain."

In the true sense of the term Mr. Knowlton is a *Pioneer*. He cleared much of the forests that stood on the seventy acres which he
purchased around the homestead,—helped dig
the canal and wheeled the dirt himself; looked
from his home at night when only five lights
could be seen in the neighborhood—and those
proceeding from old fashioned tallow-drip
candles; made the first plat or sub-division
and called it *Cumminsville*, in memory of
David Cummins from whom he bought eight
acres; was its first Postmaster; built the old
Mill Creek House at which the polls were held
when General Harrison was elected President
—at which time Mill Creek township embraced
about one fifth of the County; in short, during
his active business life, has *shingled over about
ten acres of Cumminsville* in the construction
of homes and places of business.

Mr. Knowlton was born in Connecticut, June
1803. Four score years are settling down
upon his head—and yet he is in active business
and lives at ease in an antiquated homestead
built by another over sixty years ago, and
standing upon an eminence,

"Green and of mild declivity,"

over-looking the scenes of his earlier and successful struggles to acquire a competence for
the evening of life.

A VIEW OF THE VALLEY,

From Col. Thompson's Hill, west of Cumminsville, is thus decribed by Prof. Turrill:
"A few minutes' drive up the College Hill
pike brings us to Parker avenue, where we
commence the ascent. Tethering our steed in
the shade of a haw bush not far from the brow,
we journey on foot to summit.
Here we observe the broad Mill Creek valley coming south from Lockland, with an average width of from three to five miles, dividing at
Ludlow Grove in two sections; the wider part
passing south-eastward toward Sharpsburg
and the Duck Creek valley, keeping nearly its
full width, but only about two-thirds of its
depth, all the way to the Little Miami; the

other arm turning south-westward, and with a
breadth of perhaps a mile, but very much
deeper than the other, sweeping around with a
great elbow curve opposite the West Fork gap,
and then moving onward almost directly south
to the Ohio River, its narrowest portion contracting into a gorge at the foot of the Brighton
hill about one-third of a mile wide. Down this
western channel is the present bed of the creek,
changing its locality among the loose gravel
and sand at nearly every freshet.

This valley has once been plowed or scooped
out by natural causes nearly two hundred feet
deeper than it at present appears. The exact
depth at Kirby's well before reaching the limestone strata, is 168 feet. This has since been
filled with horizontal layers of sand, gravel,
broken stones, fossils, and other debris brought
from a geological region a hundred or more
miles away. Along its sides are foot-hills of
ground-up lime stone, mixed with yellow and
blue clay, evidently the dredgings of this
former basin. These foot-hills make choice
building sites, and many wealthy citizens, like
Mr. Parker and Mr. Kirby, have crowned them
with delightful homes. The city in the distance,
villages partly embowered here and there,
gardens and farms, forest-fringed hills, white

lines of roads, the shining canal, and other well known features of landscape scenery, combined with the splendor of the lengthened shadows of the sinking sun, are a few of the charms of this hillside view."

THE METHODIST EPISCOPAL CHURCH

Was built in 1833, of which the Rev. Charles Haynes is at present pastor.

Through the kindness of this congregation, the Presbyterians held services there part of the time, until they finally built their own church in 1854.

This church is called "Wright Chapel" in memory of the late Rev. John F. Wright, D. D.

THE CHRISTIAN CHURCH

Occupies almost the exact site of the old Block House, near the intersection of Knowlton street and the C. H. & D. Railroad. It is a handsome structure and is the outgrowth of a religious enterprise which dates back as far as 1832. Mrs. Justice McLean donated the land upon which it stands.

A MAMMOTH TRADITION.

The bones of huge and monstrous animals

have been found between the Miamies, if not in this particular valley. We gather some interesting information about this matter from a book edited by Judge James Hall in 1829, entitled the "Western Souvenir."

It is said that these remains greatly puzzled the naturalists and learned men. Some maintaining that they belonged to one class and some to another.

Dr. Goforth, of early Cincinnati, once had "the largest and most complete museum of these bones ever collected,"" but it seems that an English traveler, who called his name Thomas Ashe, swindled the doctor out of them and took them to England. " Mr Ashe declares," says the author, " that this *Megalonix*, or Great Lion, was precisely sixty feet in length and twenty-five feet high; that his shoulder-blade was as large as a breakfast-table; that his paw was four feet long and three feet wide; that his skull was twelve inches thick; that, his ribs being formed like the sticks of a fan, he had the power of contracting his body to a great degree, in order to make more prodigious bounds; that his figure was magnificent; his look determined, his gait stately, and his voice tremendous." One would suppose from this, that this high authority, and of

such known veracity, (?) had met one of these
animals alive, actually taken his dimensions,
and listened to the thunder of his voice. Judge
Hall rather discredits Ashe's, reliability in view
of his disreputable treatment of Dr. Goforth.

The Shawnees, who occupied this country
anciently, had a tradition that a race of animals, in ancient times, existed in these valleys,
huge, voracious, and terrible ; "that they de-
voured the beasts of the forest until the red
men were reduced to famine for the want of
game ; that the Great Spirit took pity on his
children, and seizing his lightning hurled it in
his wrath among them, until all were killed
except the big bull, who presented his forehead
to the bolts, and shook them off as they fell,
until missing one, at last, it wounded him in
the side, whereupon, bellowing with rage and
fury, he bounded over the Ohio, the Wabash,
the Illinois, and finally over the great lakes,
where he is still living ; and that since that
time, they have never troubled the Indians
or molested their game."

CHAPTER XV.

HARTWELL.

THE halls of the Montezumas rest upon piles driven into marshes half buried in water. That swamp land, bordering on a magnificent lake, became the site of the city of Mexico, because of the superstition and *not of the intelligent forecast* of its founders. Prescott tells us that the ancient Aztecs led a nomadic life in that beautiful land of the Mexican valley; that after a series of wanderings and adventures, they at length halted on the South-western borders of that lake in the year 1325. They there beheld, perched on the stem of a prickly pear, which shot out from the crevice of a rock that had been washed by the waves, a royal eagle of extraordinary size and beauty, with a serpent in his talons, and his broad wings opened to the sun. They hailed this as an auspicious omen, announced by the oracle as indicating the site of the capital of the modern Mexican Republic.

The oracle of common sense indicated the site of Hartwell. Thereupon the Hamilton County House Building Association, purchased the Gares farm, consisting of 130 acres, and 40 acres from Judge Jonathan Cilley immediately on the west, the entire tract of 170 acres being bounded by Mill creek on the south ; the C. H. & D. R. R. on the west ; Section avenue on the north, and the canal on the east. At the same time Judge Cilley permitted 34 acres to be included in the plat of Hartwell. Thus 204 acres are embraced in the first plat made of this village.

THE NAME

Of Hartwell was then given to the embryonic town. Many names, and some beautiful and appropriate ones, were suggested. At that time, Mr. *John W. Hartwell* was Vice-president of the C. H. & D. Railroad. As an official he was polite and accommodating ; as a friend he was true ; as a gentleman, noble and high-minded ; but as a bachelor he was childless. Possessing these qualities—official, personal, domestic—it was determined to name this new-born municipality HARTWELL.

THE PLAT

Of the village was suggested by the way in which beautiful Glendale was laid out. It always requires presence of mind to walk the avenues of Glendale when having a definite place in view. So sometimes here.

THE SUCCESS

Of this enterprise is not now a debatable question. The judgment, good taste, and forethought of these gentlemen, in fixing upon this location, has been justified by the eminent success that has crowned their efforts.

But it has been a prolonged if not an uneventful voyage. Other similar enterprises have failed —were shipwrecked in the financial storms that have overswept this land since 1870. But this has weathered the storm. The little ship floats proudly to-day, full-rigged, in the harbor of yonder city.

Who was the Columbus that walked the quarterdeck the while? That both piloted and commanded amid misgivings of friends and counselors—sometimes amid jeers and imprecations; who steadfastly looked into the future and saw the substance of things hoped

for by many a contented resident of Hartwell
in the possession of a home ; who kept steadily
on his way until he finally discovered the port
and entered the harbor and cast anchor—
That clear, cool-headed man of faith, and hope,
and work, was DANIEL DeCAMP.

The building of this suburb has not been
carried on to its triumphant success without
the exercise of great will power and force of
character ; without tireless toil of body and
mind ; without, at times, an aching head,
and perchance, an aching heart—in a word,
without generalship and all that the word
implies.

His official associates ably advised, assisted
and encouraged, but it is safe to say, that but
for Mr. DANIEL DeCAMP, as President of the
Hamilton County House Building Association, Hartwell never would have been built,
at least when it was, and clothed, as it is, in the
simple majesty that now enrobes it as a suburb.

Once as he walked in meditation these pleasant avenues

—" A moment o'er his face
A tablet of unutterable thoughts
Was traced ; and then it faded as it came."

One who saw him then imagined that he was

thinking of an ancient King who once walked upon the high, broad walls that encircled his capital in the distant plains of Shinar, and looking with conscious pride upon " Its temples, its palaces, its fortresses, its brazen gates, its enamelled brick, its plated pillars, its huge embankments along the shores of the Euphrates, its artificial mountains, as high as the dome of St. Peter's, its ornamental architecture, its artificial lakes, and its lofty palaces, with its hanging gardens filled in successive terraces to the top of its walls, 300 feet high and 75 feet wide and enclosing 200 square miles," said to himself :

" Is not this great Babylon that I have built by the might of my power and for the honor of myself ?"

MAPLEWOOD.

This is the beautiful name given by Joseph F. Mills, Esq., to his popular sub-division. The boundaries are, Section avenue on the south, Burns avenue on the west, Mills avenue on the north and the Canal on the east, comprising about 100 acres. This was the old Sturgis farm, the homestead being the present residence of Mr. James S. Zerbe. That old

Farm within 90 years, a wilderness, a farm, a suburb, caught in the eddying current of the all-embracing whirl-pool of Cincinnati!

This splendid property came wholly into the possession of Mr. Mills about twelve years ago. It was sub-divided in 1871. He has expended by way of grading the streets and lots, in setting out shade and evergreen trees, since that time, (not to speak of the original investment, the amount expended in building, and the cost of constant superintendence), more than $30,000. The conversion of this farm into this beautiful hamlet in so short a time is a marvel—such as can only be effective by the possession of wealth, and a judicious, artistic, tasteful use of it.

This suburb is located in the north-eastern part of the corporation of Hartwell. Wayne avenue passes through it on the east, from north to south : Burns avenue, from north to south on the west. Both railroads pass through it. The Maplewood Depot is on the north line. The taste of an artist, the touch of the landscape gardener, the skill of the architect, and the lavish expenditure of money, have all been employed to throw this splendid picture upon nature's canvas. Its wide-spead and enviable reputation as a place for suburban homes is justified by the success of the undertaking, and by the class of citizens resident there.

Every street in this sub-division is graded and finished, set out with shade trees ten years old. Every lot, as yet unimproved, is ornamented with elms and maples and evergreens, and carpeted with green grass.

The residences are tasteful and so varied in architectural designs, and so disposed as to produce the most pleasing effects. The view up Williams avenue from Lawn is one that recalls Euclid avenue in Cleveland. To stand at the intersection of Sturgis and Central avenue and look to the four points of the compass, is to obtain a view at once unique and beautiful. Lombardy poplars in their processional alignment on either side of those avenues, and crossing each other at this point, seem like so many nodding plumes when stirred by the evening breeze. To the east may be seen the Reading Hills crowned by Notre Dame Convent; to the north Wayne Avenue M. E. Church and its duplicate spires; to the west the pretty little Episcopal Church; to the south, the new County Infirmary at Carthage. Maplewood is a consummate villa. As such it has isolation—individuality.

Without fences, the houses seem to stand as
in an immense park and in approaching it you
naturally look for a magnificent Gate Lodge to
mark the place of exit and of entrance.

It is canopied by the municipal corporation
of Hartwell, and with respect to that it is
sometimes called the Maplewood Ward.

But it nevertheless preserves and doubtless
ever will maintain certain village characteristics—ever will be called Maplewood—ever will
bear the impress of its founder and builder,
whose taste conceived its plan and beautified
it, and whose wealth enabled him, seemingly
out of affection for his departed companion, to
build this suburb as in some sense a monument
to her memory upon the ancestral lands of
Mrs. Joseph F. Mills.

THE BELL AND STEELE SUB-DIVISION.

This handsome sub-division is most advantageously surrounded—on the east Burns
avenue; on the south Section avenue; on
the east Glendale avenue; on the north the
south corporation line of Wyoming.

A portion of this tract of ground was included
in the farms belonging to the Carson heirs, Mr.
Lohman, Warren Warner and Mr. Sharpshare.

Some of the old buildings (re-modeled) are
still standing as landmarks of a past generation. Remnants of an old apple orchard;
evergreens, tall and aged, the old Sharpshare
home—once a pretentious mansion—are some
of the reminders of the days when the husband men went forth to scatter seed and gather
the harvest from the rich and fruitful fields.

The encroaching suburb of Hartwell from
the south; bright young Maplewood springing
into being on the east, and proud and wealthy
Wyoming marching southward, so enhanced
this property in value that attention was at
length called to its desirability for sub-division
into village lots. Schools, depots, churches
were on every hand. There was an eye to
see, and a head to plan, and a will to execute,
and so in time this property passed under the
control of the Merchants and Manufacturers
Building Association, of which Charles M.
Steele, Esq., was the head and front. Under
his skilful and ceaseless supervision it has
developed into the handsome property that it
now is,—in the matter of graded and shaded
streets, and in the construction of some of
the most tasteful homes in the village. The
Barger residence—elsewhere described—the
Barton, Hornbrook, Blackburn, Marpe, Shu-

mard, Wilson, Skardon and Decker residences,
are upon it, as also the present pleasant home
of Mr. Steele, who was the first mayor of
Hartwell and served as such until spring of
1881, having been twice re-elected. His administration was characterized by zeal, fidelity
and intelligence. Many of the public improvements of the village were projected and
consumated during his official career.

A RELIC.

Mr. Steele has in his possession a fluted column preserved from the old Symmes mansion,
built of blue limestone, and that, until recently,
stood on the south-east corner of Pearl and
Lawrence streets. It was one of the first—and
perhaps the finest—houses built outside of the
enclosures of old Fort Washington. In looking
upon it, we could not but ask:

> " Whose arch or pillar meets me in the face,
> Titus or Trajan's? No, 'tis that of time:
> Triumph, arch, pillar, all he doth displace
> Scoffing."

THE PRESENT MUNICIPAL OFFICES

Are: Mayor, G. V. Stevenson; Clerk, Theodore Marpe ; Treasurer, Theudas Hoge ; Marshal, John W. Carey; Assistant Marshal, Adam Friend ; Sealer of Weights and Measures, Col. T. E. McNamara ; Council, Michael Levoy, L. B. Hancock, L. S. Cumback, P. Y. Brown, John D. Burgess, and M. V. B. Weighell.

Capt. Marpe has served as clerk of this corporation since its organization. Promptitude, neatness, ability and affability have characterized his management of the office.

THE TAX DUPLICATE.

The first cost of the grounds included in the lines of the corporation under the Symmes purchase, was 66⅔ cents per acre, or about $267.00, assuming that there are exactly 400 acres. The tax duplicate for 1880 amounted to $351,352. It is safe to say that this is a low valuation.

THE POPULATION

Ascertained by the United States Census of 1880 and officially reported is 881. This includes the territory in the sub-school district outside of the corporation.

THE METHODIST CHURCH

Combines the Gothic and Swiss methods of architecture in its construction, for which it is much admired. Sometimes it is affectionately called "THE LITTLE BROWN CHURCH."

With accustomed forethought, President De Camp, of the Hamilton County House Building Association, reserved the park in the centre of the village for at least two churches, and their parsonages or rectories. The location of places of worship was in his mind in the beginning. So to this sacred reservation all the streets of Hartwell proper were made to converge.

When it was determined by the people of Hartwell and vicinity to build this church, that association, true to its implied promise, cheerfully donated that portion of the park upon which it now stands, and contributed liberally to its construction.

It was completed about six years ago at a cost, including furniture, etc., of $7,000. And it is free from indebtedness, mortgage or otherwise.

We may not name all who have contributed so lavishly of their means for its erection, but we may justifiably say that the community and

that congregation owe the conception and construction of so beautiful a temple, at that time,
to the munificent contribution and tireless en-
deavors in its behalf of CHARLES M. STEELE,
Esq. *He launched that ship of faith.*

Yet there was a rock in the way of its spiritual progress: it was heavily mortgaged. But
at length that was cancelled from the records;
and it was the liberal proposition of the mort-
gagee, superinduced by the friendly interposi-
tion of Mr. Steele, that made the final liquida-
tion of the indebtedness possible. It was the
crowning work of the three years pastorate
of the Rev. J. F. Conrey to raise the money,
through the prompt and liberal response of
the community, with which to pay and to discharge this great burden.

Rev. H. C. Weakley is now pastor in charge.

THE CHURCH OF THE HOLY TRINITY

Has a lovely and accessible location on
the south-east corner of Burns and Central
avenues. In point of architectural design
it is a baffling study. Therefore we say
that it is incomparably beautifully grotesque
as to its exterior; while within there is a dim
religious light over altar and chancel and pews,

filling the aisles and the fretted vault. It is indeed a solemn little chapel, most befittingly adapted to the worship of Him who is invisible. The upbuilding of this little pearl colored church with so little effort, and so speedily, is the source of "divine surprise" both to its communicants and to the community. The entire cost was about $3,000, which has been paid. Not a dollar of incumbrance is upon it. It is therefore in the broadest sense dedicated to the worship of God. The ground upon which it stand, was donated by Joseph F. Mills, Esq.

> "Ah, well! God grant, when with aching feet,
>   We tread life's last few paces,
> That we may hear some accents sweet,
>   And kiss to the end fond faces.
> God grant that this tired flesh may rest,
>   (Mid many a musing mourner,)
> While the sermon is preached, and the rites are read,
>   In no church where the heart of love is dead,
> But in some sweet nook where God's confessed—
>   Some little church round the corner."

The official board consists of the following named gentlemen:

Mr. Michael Levoy,   H. H. Tatem, Esq.
Mr. F. M. Whitelaw,   W. F. Armstrong, Esq.
Dr. C. R. Taft.   George Ward, Esq.
        Rev. J. H. Ely, Rector.

THE PUBLIC SCHOOL

Is in a most flourishing condition. The school building, consisting of three large rooms, but still inadequate to the wants of the community, is located on a shaded lot on North Crescent avenue. The trustees have adopted the Cincinnati method of gradations. The last yearly examination was highly creditable both to teachers and pupils. The enrollment was 114, and the average per cent. of scholarship above 70 was 81.7.

Prof. J. Harry Lowe is at present principal.

The following gentlemen compose the School Board:

Col. T. E. McNamara,
Maj. Geo. W. Cormany,
Mr. Michael Levoy.

THE HARTWELL DEPOT.

On the C. H. & D. Railroad, is located at the intersection of Burns and Cilley avenues, and at the western terminus of Park avenue. This depot is considered one of the most convenient and comfortable within, and attractive without, on any of the railroads leading to the city.

It cost about $4,000, this fund being contributed in about equal shares by the late Judge Cilley, and the Hamilton County House Building Association. The plan was drawn by Mr. Daniel DeCamp, who superintended its construction.

Mr. J. N. Bachelor is the agent in charge, and it is due him to say that he faithfully attends to his duties.

Its waiting rooms, especially for ladies, are made inviting by the keen oversight of Mrs. Bachelor. People who are about to take the train, as a rule, do not fully appreciate the efforts put forth to make their hasty call agreeable ; but nevertheless, there should always be a manifest appreciation of an incessant effort, on the part of our station agents, to make us comfortable while making this enforced call upon them.

MAPLEWOOD DEPOT

Was built originally by Mr. Joseph F. Mills. It is a model structure with pleasant waiting-rooms in the first, and living apartments in the second story.

Mr. and Mrs. A. J. Chapman are in charge, and are attentive and accommodating to pas-

sengers, and keep the place in the most creditable manner. Flower beds nestle close to each
end of the building, and a little park extends
to the south. This depot also accommodates
the lower portion of Wyoming. Many com-
muters and their families who live just across
the corporation line in Wyoming regularly take
the trains at this station.

THE LEVOY PLACE,

Known as "Valley View," is the home of MR.
and MRS. MICHAEL LEVOY. The house, in
the nomenclature of architects, would doubtless
be classified as a " Structural Park Residence."
It stands upon a lot of surpassing beauty,
fronting 200 feet on the south side of Park
avenue, and extending back 365 feet, enclosing about two acres.

This miniature park is under as high a state
of cultivation as it is possible to bring that
much of the surface of the earth. A stroll
around and through it, gives to the beholder
impressions of " the distant aiden" that do not
evanish as dreams do. The architect may
here find a pleasurable and profitable study.
The Botanist, in gazing on the mignionette,
the camillia, the eglatine and the lily, will

experience a joy greater than that found in the " pathless woods" Amidst such a scene, one can hear Ruskin saying : " Flowers are intended for the solace of humanity ; children love them ; quiet, tender, contented people love them as they grow. They are the cottager's treasures ; and in the crowded town, mark, as with a little broken fragment of rainbow, the windows of the workers in whose hearts rests the covenant of peace."

The Epicure beholds the clusterful vine embowering its arbor-home ; the *Ribes Rubrum* in reserve in each nook and corner, or marshalled in red ranks ; the ambushed strawberry and " the esculent tuber" ; the purple plum, the hawthorn, the apple and the apricot.

Within that cultured home, the poet and the painter, the musician and the *littérateur* will meet with welcome and find companionship. Its richly papered and profusely pictured walls, the tufted carpets, the festooned windows, the books, the music and the maze of rooms, conspire. to make it as lovely a home as heart could wish.

When the mellow radiance of moon and stars falls upon VALLEY VIEW, the falling waters of Lindaraxa are only wanting to completely realize Irving's immitable description of a moonlight night in Andalusia.

THE TATEM RESIDENCE

Presents a beautiful type of the American Cottage Villa—an architectural gem set and sequestered beneath old elms and beeches, and amid rare plants and shrubbery. The house is approached along a carriage way, so beset with trees that you do not fully take in its lovely outlines and situation until you are nearly up to it. "The Beeches" is the chosen name of this pretty place, and is owned and occupied by CAPT. AND MRS. H. H. TATEM. The elegant Barber mansion adjoins it on the south, and Spinning's splendid grounds on the north. It fronts on Woodbine avenue, the ground rising to the west,

"Where blossoms many an incense bearing tree;
And here are beeches, ancient as the hills,
Infolding sunny spots of greenery."

Passing the threshold, the eye falls upon solid gold papered walls; upon floors concealed beneath elegant druggets; upon windows curtained by costly laces; upon pictures and paintings, choice and rare; mottoed mantles carved in wood and resting upon delicately tiled hearthstone; upon statuary in bronze and Parian marble; upon books, adapted to the taste of the literary epicure, whether poet, philosopher, scientist, or statesman ; the lover of history or romance.

Once—

> " It was in the bleak December,
> And each separate dying ember
> Wrought its ghost upon the floor."—

The guest of the evening wheeled a cushioned seat in front of the slumberous grate,

> " Then into the velvet sinking
> He betook himself to linking,
> Fancy unto fancy thinking,—
> With his head at ease reclining
> On the cushions velvet lining
> That the lamplight gloated o'er."

THE STEVENSON PLACE,

In style, is the Gothic Villa Americanized, and is the elegant home of COL. G. V. STEVENSON, Mayor of Hartwell. It is located on the corner of Park and Eastern avenues, fronting south and east. The *tout ensemble* of the residence can not be here advantageously described. It is a painting from a master's hand.

The lawn is bedecked with flowers and enlivened with their varied colors. Here are grouped the Arbor Vita, the Spruce, the Pine and the Hemlock: there the Cornus Aba, the Spirea, the Deutzia and the Japonica; here the maple and the elm cast their blended shadows on the ground; and there the apple and cherry and pear let their ripening fruitage fall upon the lap of earth.

Amidst such a scene the house rises like a thing of beauty, with its exterior outline broken by porches and piazzas, by hooded and bay windows, by frieze and architrave and cornice. The painting is exquisite—the colors so blending from old gold to Indian red as to charm the eye. This home is distinguished for its interior decorations, especially in the line of artistic wall paper. Marston's "raw silk and tapestry copies," "embossed and gilt," are called into requisition. Costly pictures, paintings, bronzes, plaques, &c., selected with consummate taste, profusely abound. Books and periodicals and papers load the tables and shelves.

> " Around that hearth by night
>   What gladsome looks of household love
>   Meet in the ruddy light.
>   Then woman's voice flows forth in song,
>   Or childish tale is told,
>   *Or lips move mournfully along*
>   *The warrior's woes to unfold.*

THE STEELE RESIDENCE

Is the handsome home of MR. AND MRS.
CHARLES M. STEELE. It is situated on the
south-west corner of Highland and Burns
avenues, having a beautiful eastern view to the
front, and indeed, in all directions. The lot
is in a high state of cultivation, being ornamented with flower beds and young shade
trees, and having a sward as level as a floor.
This property has great advantages as to location, it being but a square from the Maplewood
depot. The Episcopal Church is immediately
south of it; the southern corporation line of
Wyoming is within one square to the north;
while to the north extends Burns avenue
through the prettiest part of Wyoming. The
churches and public schools of that village are
but a remove from it, and the splendid residence of Loring Hinsdale, Esq., and Major
Armstrong are in close proximity.

Along Burns avenue, carriages, phaetons,
and all kinds of pleasure equipages, are constantly passing, thus rendering that location a
public and yet a pleasurable one.

The house has an attractive appearance
without, and seems to wear a cheerful smile.
The arrangement within is faultless for the

size of the house. Its walls are beautifully papered and an air of taste and refinement pervades it.

The transformation of this acre of farmland into the cultured lawn and tasteful dwelling place, in so short a time, is another instance illustrative of the magical growth of our valley.

"I would have, then, our ordinary dwelling houses built to last and built to be lovely; as rich and full of pleasantness as may be within and without, with such differences as might suit and express each man's character and occupation and partly his history; raising thus the habitation into a kind of monument, and developing that good custom which was of old universal and which still remains with some of the Swiss and Germans, of acknowledging God's permission to build and possess a quiet resting place."

THE WICK RESIDENCE

Has a pleasant location between South Crescent and Oak avenues, extending from one to the other.

This comfortable, unpretentious house was built by the Hamilton County House Building Association, and is now occupied by MR. AND MRS. C. C. WICK.

The two railroads between which it is located, seem to converge in its front, thus adding this stirring feature to the lovely landscape. The steeples, domes and towers of the fair grounds, gas hall, school buildings, churches, state and county charitable institutions, rise majestically in view among and above the rich, dark-green foliage of trees, the whole forming a wonderful scene, and a source of the purest pleasure when contemplated from the shaded porch of his village home.

The chief feature within doors is the classical musical library. Here Mendelssohn, Handel, Beethoven, Mozart, Wagner, Liszt, and other great composers, live and move and have their being, in their deathless harmonies.

> " Here music dwells,
> Lingering and wandering on, as loth to die,
> Like thoughts whose very sweetness yieldeth proof
> That they were born for immortality."

Madame De Stael said that " architecture is frozen music." Be it so.

The music of these great composers, within many and many a humble home, compensates largely for the absence of the frozen frieze and congealed cornice without.

Companionship with these song masters;

led by them through tuneful worlds of their
creation, and thrilled by strains, forever new,
that fall from their divine harps, it is no won-
der that one of earth's greatest poets sighed—

> "O that I were the viewless spirit of a lovely sound;
> A living voice, a breathing harmony!
> Born and dying with the blest tone that made me."

It is no marvel that, possessing their works,
the quiet leader of the village band should so-
liloquise with the rightful Duke of Milan:

> "Me, poor man!—my library,
> Is dukedom large enough for me."

THE WEIGHELL RESIDENCE

Is another beautiful model of an American
home. It is most eligibly located, midway between the two stations, on the south-east corner of Park and south Cresent avenues, and
kept in perfect order from sidewalk to foundation stones, from foundation stones to turret.
No expense has been spared to make it so. It
has a curvilinear front of 220 feet on Park by
600 feet on Cresent avenues, and encloses
about three acres of the choicest ground in the
village. It commands splendid views in every

direction. The lot is embellished with choice
plants and flowers, and young forest trees, and
a lawn as smooth as nature's floor can be
made.

The interior of the house is its chief and
most valuable feature. It is imposing. The
spacious double parlor, wide, extended hall,
library, and reception and dining rooms, and
the concomitant pantries, the area of cellar and
its appointments, all tend to make it a superbly
convenient dwelling place. And then the entire furnishment with which those floors are
carpeted, those walls beautified, those rooms
filled with elegant furniture and paintings !

> " A charm from the skies seems to hallow us here,
> Which seek through the world,
> Is ne'r meet with elsewhere."

Such is the home of MR. and MRS. M. V.
B. WEIGHELL, member of the village council.

THE BARBER MANSION,

Now occupied by MR. AND MRS. JOHN C.
MOORE, is a beautiful type of suburban home,
and is the property of Mr. J. W. Barber.
The lot is undulatory and sweeps like a green
wave from Woodbine to Ohio avenue on the

west. The grounds have been graded and
embellished at great expense. The pleasures
of home are evidenced in the varied plants and
shrubs—the walks, the summer houses, the
cool embankments of ferns, and the old over-
shadowing trees. The judgment of a con-
noisseur selected the pictures that adorn the
interior walls, and the artistic hand of a
daughter has found therein an *atelier*.

Looking at "Moses," as painted by that
artiste, we realized the truth of these words:

"Painting is a noble and expressive language, and invaluable as a vehicle of thought.
Its excellences are what rhyme, melody, pre-
cision and force are in the words of the orator
and poet."

THE HON. THEODORE MARSH'S RESIDENCE

Is a noble type of the village mansion, it
bears the name of "The Lone Oak." The
house, half unseen amid the trees that em-
bower it, seems almost smothered by the
trellised honeysuckle and the latticed colum-
bine.

The "Lone Oak"—that king of the juvenile
forest, stands like a sentinel between "that
loved home and the storm's desolation."

The sward, so level and so green, looks as
if it had never yielded to the sickle, nor resounded to the ploughman's tread.

Byron had in his mind such a home as this
when he wrote :

"'Tis sweet to hear the watch-dog's honest bark,
   Bay deep-mouthed welcome as we draw near home ;
'Tis sweet to know there is an eye will mark
Our coming, and will look brighter when we come.

MRS. MARGARET KNIGHT'S RESIDENCE

Has an air of retiracy and repose indispensable to a suburban home. The stately man-
sion-like house stands back on a splendid lot,
with a sweeping frontage curving gracefully
to the South to conform to the boundaries of
the village park, which is in its immediate
front. From its hearthstone may be heard,
perhaps too distinctly, the hum and roar of
passing trains, or the ceaseless march and
counter-march of humanity over the stoneless
streets of the village. A pebbled carriage
way sweeps as a semi-circle in front of the
house, along which flowers breathe their perfume, and rare plants and shrubbery are taste-
fully disposed so as to relieve the green sward
of its seeming monotony. Without it com-

mands admiration, while within it is fault-
lessly arranged and elaborately furnished.

Certainly a quiet retreat for its venerable
resident owner, from which to watch the setting sun and dawning stars, so typical of the
evening of life and the coming of a brighter
and better to-morrow.

THE LOWES RESIDENCE

Is a splendid home, located on the south side
of Mystic avenue. The natural elevation of
the ground above this avenue is a valuable
feature. This house is conspicuously seen
from the eastern hills and from passing trains,
and is admired for its pleasing architecture.
Beneath that drooping willow may be obtained
as cool and invigorating well-water as ever
quenched human thirst. Recent additions
have been made to the house by way of piazzas, bay-windows, summer-houses, etc., the
whole constituting the home of MR. AND MRS.
JAMES A. LOWES.

MR. JAMES R. WILLIAMS' RESIDENCE.

This is an ornamental cottage with a Southern front on Park and Mystic avenues. When

approached from Mystic avenue, the lot rises to
an eminence, and has a gentle elevation when
viewed from Park avenue.

Mr. Thomas Gibson, of Cincinnati, owns this
property, and it is occupied by MR. AND MRS.
JAMES R. WILLIAMS.

" When the day goes away and the shadows
of the evening are stretched out," the steeple
of the Methodist church throws its shadow
across this wide-spreading lawn, so near is the
chosen place of worship to the denizens of this
pretty country home.

MR. JACOB T. SPINNING'S RESIDENCE.

Surrounding the house is a remnant of the
primeval forest just as the Indian, doubtless,
saw it a century ago, save that the underbrush
has been supplanted by flowering plants and
shrubs. The trees remain. Dusky maidens
no more wait for warrior lovers beneath that
aged elm. "Pale faces" now read and re-
cline there. Instead of "the sharp twang and
the deadly whir of the loaded arrow, followed
by the dull, drear echo of a bolt that smites
its mark," the polished shafts of accomplished
archers speed on their harmless way, as may be
witnessed on a summer evening when Col.

W. P. Wiltsee, as a modern Cambyses with a Macrobian bow, and as chief of an Archery tribe, drills his braves and their maidens in the Sagittarian art on the green and level lawn.

*COL. T. E. M'NAMARA'S

Home in the center of Maplewood, deserves especial mention as a representative of this beautiful young suburb.

It is a square-built, substantial and handsome structure, almost severe in the simplicity of its design, exhibiting in its construction a regard for comfort rather than showiness, and yet it is one of the few home spots in the village whose striking character and surroundings, ample, well kept grounds, covered with shrubbery, and in their season, radiant and redolent with flowers, inevitably attract the attention of the passer-by.

To Col. McNamara belongs the distinction of being the pioneer of Maplewood. His was the first residence erected and occupied in the village, which was then a bare field without trees, graded streets or other improvement, and

---

* Mr. McNamara is at present serving as aid-de-camp with the rank of Colonel, upon the staff of GOVERNOR CHARLES FOSTER.

it is worthy of remark that upon this very
spot at one time stood the wigwam home of
the Indians, as may be fairly presumed from
the fact that when Williams avenue (in its front)
was graded, ashes, shells, beads, arrow-heads,
and mouldering bones, were exhumed, affording almost indubitable evidence of the fact that
this

> " Lone and pleasant dell
> This valley in the west "

was an encampment, if not a burial place, for
another and a departed race.

> " The statesman, lawyer, merchant, man of trade,
> Pants for the refuge of some rural stade,
> Where, all his long anxieties forgot,
> He dwells midst charms of a sequestered spot."

DR. W. H. BUNKER

Has a splendid residence on the north side of
Cilley avenue, built in the decorated suburban
style, with vines festooning its porches and
shrubbery ornamenting its lawn.

Upon such a porch, shaded by such vines
and pleased with such views—Aurora Leigh

> " Would gloriously forget herself
> And plunge, soul-forward, headlong,
> Into a book's profound,"

MR. L. B. EATON

Has just erected a new building on Ohio and Park avenues, intended for his residence and a public store. He is postmaster of the village.

MR. S. B. KELLY'S

Beautiful residence in Maplewood, so distinctly seen from many a standpoint in this valley, should be mentioned in this connection as showing the development in house architecture in this vicinity. It is a noble specimen of a house in the Elizabethan villa style, being a two-story frame with porches, bay-windows and a tower. The lot is a spacious one, covered with a choice variety of flowers and shrubbery—the wild tulip being one of its most pleasing features. The interior of this mansion comports in every respect with its delightful exterior.

Its walls are all richly decorated with pictures and paintings, the whole suggesting comfort and refinement.

The view from the tower of this house is remarkably pleasing. It illustrates the words of Tupper :

"O blinded is the eye, if it see not just aptitude in all things,
O frozen is the heart, if it glow not with gratitude for all
  things,
In the perfect circle of creation not an atom could be spared
From earth's magnetic zone to the bind-weed 'round a
  hawthorne."

THE OLD GARES HOMESTEAD,

Now the remodeled residence of L. B. Cook,
Esq., stands on a large and beautiful lot on
Park avenue. It was once the center of a farm
—now it is the center of a remnant acre. It
stands amidst full grown trees, than which it is
older. It was built by the Greenham family,
more than sixty years ago, so that its complete
history, there is probably none living to tell.
He who laid its foundation stones, and he who
moulded the brick out of which its old walls
were constructed, have themselves doubtless
fallen asleep in the slumber of death.   But
the old walls, and the new addition just completed, still constitute a pleasant home ; and
in and out of the old doorway generations may
yet pass before it shall cease to turn upon its
old fashioned hinges.

THE KOEHLER HOMESTEAD

Possesses the characteristics of a land mark.

A wealthy gentleman named John D. Gettis built it for his private country residence about forty years ago. He was a Yankee adventurer and began his career in New Orleans as a drayman; subsequently acquired wealth, married a daughter of Mr. John D. Harris, a pioneer in this valley, and passed much of his time in this, then elegant home.

An artificial lake was in front of this house fed by an upland spring and the little rivulet that still flows at the foot of the hill.

The house now wears a mournful look. Magnificent old evergreens stands round it as if mantling its fading splendors, while the beautiful fields roll in green waves in all directions from it, as the billows of the sea sometimes roll away from a mastless and masterless ship

"Rocked in the cradle of the deep."

This property (with the farm upon which it stands) now belongs to MRS. ELIZABETH KOEHLER.

A DEER STORY.

Mrs. Jane Wilmuth, (now a resident of Wyoming, a sketch of whom appears in the chapter on that village) relates this story : Her father, William Evitt, who lived at the time (1813) in a log cabin where the Ruffner house now stands on Wayne avenue, just south of the Methodist church, shot at and wounded a deer in the vicinity of his cabin (then a dense woods). The deer bounded bleeding away, but was tracked by the dog and little Jane to the banks of Mill creek, near the present crossing of Wayne avenue in Hartwell, where it was found dead.

THE ST. CLAIR HOUSE.

In an early day (about 1832), Arthur St. Clair, Jr., occupied a small house on the northeastern part of the Bogen farm. The building stood but a short time, when from some cause it took fire and burned down. The house was immediately rebuilt and some of the timber of the old was used in the construction of the new. This still stands and may be seen to the west of the pike a few hundred feet, and not far south of the Compton road.

A TRADITION.

In the south-east corner of Major G. W. Cormany's lot, on the west of Hartwell, once stood an old frame house. The location may be identified by a group of locust trees still standing there. This house was taken down at an early day and the frame work removed and rebuilt into a house upon the knoll to the west, still seen and occupying a position about the center of Rensselaer Park, formerly known as the Cilley farm. The walls were painted in a remarkable way. One side of the house represented a plantation scene—a Southern home, with a beautiful lady descending broad steps that led down to a lawn where lounged and waited slaves—a scene decidedly characteristic of the days of slavery.

Another wall represented a forest with Indians lurking therein and the primeval cabin with its curling smoke and coonskin adornments fastened against the outer wall.

These paintings were supposed to represent the *savage* and the *civilized* state of our people at that stage of American society.

There is a well authenticated tradition that Arthur St. Clair, son of Governor St. Clair, used to resort to this spot, and amuse himself in playing upon his violin.

RESIDENTS.

The following persons have likewise con-

tributed to the development of the valley by
providing themselves with pleasant homes in
this village :

F. M. Whitelaw, Esq.	L. B. Hancock, Esq.
Jeremiah Faulkner.	Benjamin Barton, Esq.
Herman Mohring.	P. Y. Brown, Esq.
Mr. James J. Burgess.	J. M. Marston, Esq.
Col. James D. Welsh.	Mr. Frank Wilson.
William Leeper, Esq.	Frank Bloomer, Esq.
Mr. A. B. Shumard.	Mrs. G. W. Kerr.
Chas. S. Wiltsee, Esq.	R. P. Thompson, Esq.
Mr. H. P. Pflume,	Prof. Carl G. Huber.
Mrs. Helen Russell.	Mr. William Ewing.
Mr. John P. Mace.	Joseph A. Reckner,Esq
Mr. Wm. F. Mitchell.	Mr. Charles H. Rust.
Mr. Wm. Moffett.	Capt. T. H. Marpe.
Mr. Philip Krug.	John W. Hill, Esq.
Mr. Henry A. Hills.	Mr. Theudas Hoge.
Mr. O. E. Connor.	Mrs. Caroline Healy.
Mr. A. Herbolshimer.	H. D. Blackburn, Esq.
A. J. DeCamp, Esq.	J. M. C. Gates, Esq.
John W. Friend, Esq.	Mr. F. G. Gerwig.
Mr. Lyman DeCamp.	Mrs. Job. DeCamp.
G. W. Crouse, Esq.	Maj. L. S. Cumback.
D. W. Conrey, Esq.	Mr. John Skillman.
J. D. Burgess, Esq.	Mr. A. E. Clark.
E. G. Warman, Esq.	Chas. W. Jones, Esq.

Robert Morrison, Esq.   B. F. Wright, Esq.
Richard Hombrook.   J. W. Barger, Esq.
Robert Keith, Esq.   J. P. Harris, Esq.
L. B. Eaton, Esq.   L. E. Brown, Esq.
Mr. W. C. Johnson.   Mrs. Joanna DeCamp.
Mr. A. Martin.

ELMWOOD.

Derives its name from an old elm standing on the south line of the village—an elm so aged that it doubtless was a beautiful young tree one hundred years ago.

In looking at it, the words of James Russell Lowell, suggests themselves to the mind :

> " A little of thy steadfastness,
> Rounded with leafy gracefulness,
> Old Elm give me ;
> That the world's blasts around me blow,
> And I yield gently to and fro,
> While my stout hearted trunk below
> And firm set roots unshaken be."

This village has had a marvellous growth—perhaps no part of the valley has more rapidly developed than this. The advance from 66⅔ cents to $4,000 per acre, since the date of the Symmes purchase, is an astonishing instance

of increase in values. It stands upon historic
ground. General Wayne and his soldiers encamped almost upon this exact locality and
marched across it in 1793.

The incident related under the title " Bloody
Run " (page 61) occurred at the little stream
just south of the village. It is but a remove
from the north corporation line of Cincinnati,
and soon may be absorbed within its limits.
The facilities for reaching the city are great,
and yet it is so located as to appear utterly removed from its contact, while its surrounding
scenery, especially to the west, presents a
beautiful landscape.

This sub-division has been under the energetic management of Mr. A. G. Bofinger and
Lewis C. Hopkins, Esq.

The Dayton Short Line Railroad passes
directly through it, and the C. H. & D. Railroad immediately to the west. It is less than
two miles from the north corporation line of
the city, from the center of which it is nine
miles by rail and five by the pike.

The ground was purchased directly from
Franklin C. Whetstone and was originally the
Anthony Cook farm. It was first laid out in
town lots in April 1876. The first lots sold in
the village were numbered 131 and 132 to Mr.

C. W. Withenbury, and 161 and 162 to Mr. C. E. Babbitt. The first house was built August 1876 by Mr. Isaac Cook at the corner of Township and Elm avenues. In April 1878, seventeen acres were added to this sub-division known as the Orchard property. The first marriage in the place was that of Mr. Frances Wenz to Miss Alice Russell, July 25, 1877. The first birth was that of Walter Elmwood Chapman, son of *C. Bart and Sarah B. Chapman, which occurred October 6, 1877.

The Union Sabbath school was established in the Short Line Depot, June 2, 1878, with forty-one scholars and is still in a flourishing condition. In the same place regular weekly meetings have been held. During the present year a Union Chapel will be built. The post-office was established June 5, 1879, with Mrs. Mary A. Hund as postmistress, and the first mail received August 7, 1879.

---

*We are indebted to Mr. Chapman for these "first things" in Elmwood.

CHAPTER XVI.

PARK PLACE.

Occupies a situation of great natural beauty on the C. H. & D. Railroad, about twelve miles from the city. It was laid out in 1876 by the Park Place Land Association of which Mr. Grant H. Burrows is the energetic president.

That it has grown to its attractive proportions and is so successful an enterprise, is mainly due to his acknowledged business enterprise and foresight. Park Place is a beautiful village —the offspring of Wyoming and yet looking towards Glendale as its alien mother and to Woodlawn as a sister. The avenues are located with reference to the contour of the ground. The plan of the village is unique. Its residences are of a varied and superior order of architecture. The Springfield turnpike passes through the centre of it. The depot is a quaint specimen of architecture, but always admired. It rises almost upon the site of the old saw mill that passed away more than fifty years ago.

The Allen homestead is the principal feature of this suburb. One hundred acres were absorbed by the company, leaving eight acres for this homestead—the pleasant, hospitable home of MR. AND MRS. EDWARD P. ALLEN.

Mr. Edward E. Townley owns and occupies a conspicuous and tasteful home in the center of the village and upon its highest point.

We notice the residences also, of Col. J. H. Thornton, Mr. M. B. Farrin, Alfred Hess, Esq. Mr. Geo. R. Shafer, Lewis A. Zeiler, Esq. and Mr. J. F. Meyer.

CAMP JOHN M'LEAN.

The 75th Ohio Infantry was recruited on the farm of Edward P. Allen, Esq., (now Park Place) in the summer of 1861. The encampment was named in honor of Justice John Mc-Lean, of the United States Supreme Court and father of Colonel N. C. McLean. It gathered into its ranks many of the noblest young men of this valley, and indeed, with this regard, it may be called the " Mill Creek Valley " Regiment, for it was largely recruited from this territory. Glendale was represented by *Col. N. C. McLean and Capt. Elias

*Subsequently promoted to brigadier-general.

R. Monfort; Hamilton, by Henry L. Morey
now a Member of Congress from that District;
Wyoming, by Col. Robert Reily and
Col. C. W. Friend; Lockland, by Major
Geo. B. Fox and Lieut. W. H. H. Dumont—
besides having gallant representatives in many
non-commissioned officers and privates.

A summary of the distinguished services of
this regiment is given as pertaining to the history of this valley. From that camp went
forth about one thousand men in bright uniforms,
with flags and drums; with heavy but brave
hearts; with many a tear dimming the eyes;
but not of remorse: — they went away—
how many hearts ached in the bosoms
of those who said " good bye " as the sound of
the distant drum told that they were indeed
gone? How many hearts ache to-day for
those who never, never will return? Is it any
marvel that now and then a wife or a mother
or sweet-heart, waited and watched for the
return, until reason fled, and madness came
which never went away? How thrilling the
story of the Drummer's Bride—

"Hollow-eyed and pale, at the window of a jail,
Through her soft disheveled hair a maniac did stare, stare,
    stare!
At a distance down the street, making music with their feet,

Came the soldiers from the wars, all embellished with their
    scars,
    To the tapping of a drum, of a drum ;
    To the pounding and the sounding of a drum !
    Of a drum, of a drum, of a drum, drum, drum, drum !
      *   *   *   *   *   *   *
Now she sees them in the street, march along with dusty feet.
And she looks through the spaces gazing madly in their
    faces ;
And she reaches out her hand screaming wildly to the band ;
But her words, like her lover, are lost beyond recover,
    ' Mid the beating of a drum, of a drum,
    ' Mid the clanging and the banging of a drum,
    Of a drum, of a drum, of a drum, drum, drum, drum.''

In January, 1862, the regiment was ordered
into Western Virginia. It was in the battle of
Monterey Court House, April 12, 1862, Stone-
wall Jackson confronted the brigade of which
it was a part near Staunton, and in this severe
battle it lost ninety killed and wounded. Was
at Cedar Mountain ; and at Graveton, near
Bull Run, April 30, it bore the whole weight
of Longstreet's corps and lost heavily in
officers and men, the colors receiving ninety
shots. At Chancellorsville the most distinguished coolness and bravery were mani-
fested by officers and men, and in one-half
hour, one hundred and fifty were killed and
wounded. This is but an epitome of their
glorious services. Is it not enough ?

WOODLAWN.

Midway between Wyoming and Glendale, and on the eastern side of Mill creek, Woodlawn occupies as elevated and eligible a site as either of the above-named suburbs.

This eminence was doubtless an important point of observation in early days, both for the Indians and the pioneers. From the point now occupied by the Lovell residence, especially from its tower, no grander or more extended view can be had of the surrounding country.

The railroad hugs its western base while the western fork of Mill creek sweeps along its southern and western sides.

Over its summit passed General Wayne's army. Wayne avenue is extended through this beautiful village, thus being a continuous thoroughfare from Hartwell, through Lockland, to Woodlawn.

Years ago Jonathan Spillman's Tavern stood on the present site of the Lovell homestead, a great resort in past times.

The arrival and departure of the old stage coach on its pilgrimages to and from Hamilton to Cincinnati is superseded by lightning express trains over an iron highway.

The old Baptist meeting-house on this hill, having served its day and generation, has been transformed into a stable.

In this vicinity, Tucker's station stood during the winter of 1792-3.

The block-house stood on the east side of the old Wayne war-trace, immediately opposite the late residence of Manning Tucker, Esq., son of Henry Tucker, the pioneer. Mr. Horace Bugher now owns the highly improved farm upon which it stood within the precincts of this village.

During the Rebellion, when Morgan's Rebel cavalry were fleeing through Glendale, a portion of his command becoming separated from it, sent up rockets from this point to indicate their whereabouts.

Upon this historic ground Woodlawn was laid out in 1876, by Thomas T. and George S. Brown, two enterprising brothers of the firm of T. T. Brown & Co., of Cincinnati.

Their first purchase and that which constitutes the village proper—the center of this extensive and wealthy neighborhood—comprises one hundred and fifteen acres of the Tucker farm.

The C. H. & D. Railroad passes directly through it, and these gentlemen have erected, at their own expense, one of the most beautiful

depots on the railroad. Much taste is mani-
fested in the style of houses erected. They
have expended altogether in improvements
about $35,000.

A new school-house has just been completed
at the expense of the township, costing $4,500.

The private residences of Mr. Thomas T.
and George S. Brown, in point of architecture, interior finish, and art decorations,
spacious and cultivated grounds, will compare
favorably with the most beautiful places in
Glendale or Wyoming. The stately homestead of Mrs. Oliver S. Lovell stands perhaps
upon the highest point in this suburb.

The property is now under the management
of the Woodlawn House Building Company,
with a capital stock of $200,000, offering special
inducements to buyers.

The board of directors consists of Thomas
T. and George S. Brown, Stephen Coles,
Levi J. Workum, Wm. W. Kelsall, Smith
Stimmel and John B. Schroeder.

There are now about thirty houses in the
village and its precincts, and 200 inhabitants.
Hon. Levi J. Workum of the firm of Freiburg
& Workum, proposes soon to build an elegant
home for himself here.

Hon. Louis Ballouf, State Senator from

Hamilton County, contemplates the erection of two fine residences.

BEAUMONT PLACE.

Standing upon the tower of the splendid residence of Mrs. Oliver Lovell, situated on one of the commanding eminences in Woodlawn, a view of the entire length of the valley may be obtained.

A frameless and boundless picture is spread out before you.

The view widens and extends in its greatest loveliness to the south. Away over the emerald ocean may be seen the azure-robed hills that look down on the Ohio from both sides of that river. You can distinctly see the Probasco and Schoenberger palaces in Clifton,

> " Where the castled crag of Drachenfels
> Frowns o'er the wide and winding Rhine,"

To the east of which may be seen Burnet Woods Park, the twin spires of Calhoun street Cathedral towering above Mount Auburn and Avondale, and marking a place of descent into the " smoke-shut battle-field " of Cincinnati.

To the right and left rise the wooded hills that look eternal, and only seem to be boundaries or shores to this sea of glory.

Within this lot stands an aged pear tree, eight feet and one inch in circumference at its base, still hale with health, and putting forth leaves from bursting buds to provide fruit, perhaps for the hundreth time, to hungering and thirsting humanity.

In planting and cultivating the vineyard many relics have been found, to-wit : a coin 141 years old, old brass buttons, evidently from some old Continental's coat, bones, beads,.etc.

CHAPTER XVII.

WYOMING.

HAMILTON County, with its Cincinnati, may not inappropriately be compared to Midlothian County, with its Edinburgh, in Scotland. And this being permissible, Wyoming might, with eminent fitness, be called the " Heart of Midlothian," although the resemblance would be more striking were there an old " Tolboth " on any of its beautiful avenues as a source of internal revenue, or a " high, antique building with turrets and iron gates," to be used as a prison within its corporate limits.

The village embraces at present about eight hundred acres of land, rising to the west from the C. H. & D. Railroad, its western limits being indicated by a ridge crowned with the splendid residences elsewhere described.

The following descriptive allusion to this location is from the pen of Captain James F. Clegg :

" If there is a lovelier stretch of country in the neighborhood of any populous American city than that portion of Mill Creek valley lying between Winton Place or Carthage and Glendale, no picturesque pencil has yet shown it; and if the center and heart of all the loveliness of this landscape should be sought, the brush of the painter and the compass of the surveyor would unite agreeably upon the one point before us. There are features of peculiar beauty about these little villages. Upon the hill-tops on the west tower some of the handsomest residences in the neighborhood of Cincinnati, while from each side of the lime-white turnpike below there are broad, green lawns and pretty terraces, and picturesque houses, and, more than all, the generous shade of great groups of old-time trees and grassy plats that even the vandal hands of business have spared. The bright, clean beeches, the maples, or sugar trees as they are more commonly called, seem exempt from the ravages of what is supposed to be a higher life. The dogwood, with its pretty blossoms, flourishes, and, later in the season, the sumach adds its luster."

THE NAME

Of Wyoming was selected at the residence of Colonel Reily, April 2d, 1861, at a meeting of his neighbors convened in response to the following invitation :

*TWIN OAKS, April 2, 1861.

Sirs:—The neighbors propose a meeting at our house for the purpose of giving a name to our embryo village, on the 4th inst., upon which occasion we hope to have the pleasure of seeing yourselves and wives. Do not fail to come with names. Ladies will be expected to participate.   Yours,

ROBERT REILY.

At the 21st anniversary, duly observed by the citizens, the Hon. Judson Harmon (Judge of the Superior Court of Cincinnati and a resident of this village), delivered a thoughtful address, from which we take the following extract :

"There are thousands of villages in the land whose history is like the history of our own, from most of which ours differs only in its suburban situation and charter so happily blending city and country that while we have not all the advantages of either, we avoid most of the discomforts of both, and from some of which we differ in true democratic spirit, which has

___

*The name given by Col. Reily to his residence, now the property of Mr. E. P. Stout. See page 115.

always prevailed among us. Wealth is enjoyed
without arrogance or vain display, and honest
poverty is no disgrace.

What expectations may we have of the
growth of our village except that her houses
may multiply, her lawns extend, her flowers
and trees increase and flourish, that no rude
sound of misery or war may ever drown
the singing of her birds—that it may never
be sung of her,

> " Sweet smiling village loveliest of the lawn,
>   Thy sports are fled and all thy charms withdrawn,
>   Amidst thy bowers the tyrant's hand is seen
>   And desolation saddens all thy green."

But while the little towns and hamlets which
dot the map of our country present to the
casual observer only this simple picture of in-
dividual and social life, is there not a silent
grandeur about them to one who looks deeper
and considers them in their relations to the
nation?   Less than one-fifth of the American
people live in the large cities.   More than
forty millions of them live in these small
places and the country surrounding them of
which they are the social capitals.   These are
real centers of national life.   They are the
ganglia of the great national nerves.   From

them the tidings of great events, through them
the throbs of popular feeling, the currents of
popular thought, the impulses of popular will,
are sent thrilling to the very tips of the nation's
life, and back through them again come surg-
ing the responsive movements of popular
action. The men, by whom the places in
which the force is applied to its object, are
called famous; but they are only trustees of a
glory which is the common property of all.

Was it Concord and Lexington, with their
few scores of men, that shook the world, or
was it thousands of other places behind them
waiting only the occasion? Was it Springfield
and Mentor, those pretty places, which gave
to the Republic her martyr Presidents, or did
the vine whose roots pervade the land merely
happen to put forth there the blossoms with
which Columbia adorned her brow?

What Concord and Lexington did, the men
Springfield and Mentor furnished, would have
been impossible then, and would be valueless
now, if every place in the land had not been
then and were not now ready to become a Concord or a Lexington, liable to become a Springfield or a Mentor.

And later in our history was it not in the
hamlet and the school district, not in Washing-

ton and New York, that the spirit rose ; was it
not from them that the power went forth, which
saved and preserved us a nation ?"

Among the earliest of these families who
followed the pioneers and settled permanently
in our neighborhood was the well-known one
of Pendery. Their grandfather and father
immigrated to the tract still owned by their
descendants, in 1805, coming down the Ohio in
keel boats lashed together with log-chains. It
is worthy of mention that Mrs. Pendery,
mother of Israel and Goodloe, was the first female white child born in the present limits of
Cincinnati. They settled on a farm of 140
acres of which forty acres were given to Mr.
Thomas Wilmuth.

Mrs. JANE EVATT WILMUTH, the oldest pioneer of Wyoming, was born August 28, 1798, in
Maryland. Her father's name was William
Evatt. He immigrated to Ohio in 1805, and
settled in the valley in the same year, building
a log cabin on the old Hamilton road, (now
Wayne avenue) near where the Ruffner house
now stands and south of the Methodist church
(Lockland). Her father died there in 1813.

The following year her widowed mother built
a log cabin upon the exact site where now
stands the Friend homestead in Wyoming. The
mother cleared three acres around her cabin,
in the raising of the same and clearing the
ground, being assisted by such pioneer neighbors as were then in this settlement. This
was about the first, probably the second, cabin
in Wyoming.

In 1815 (September 17), Jane Evatt married
Thomas Wilmuth, a widower then living in a
log cabin near the present residence of Mrs.
Wilmuth where the old well may still be seen.
This cabin was subsequently torn down and a
frame erected where her house now stands. In
1860 her husband died, aged 100 years. Three
years afterwards, one cold snowy day, her
house took fire and burned to the ground. The
sincere sympathy of her neighbors found
practical expression in a fund being immediately raised with which a better house was
built for her in a very short time. This sub-
scription was started upon the ground while
the house was burning, the list being headed
by Mr. John C. Thorpe, Esq., John H. Tangeman, R. H. Andrews, Esq., and other friends.

When a child (1807), she attended school at
the old log school-house that stood on the west

side of the pike (now Park Place), her pathway being blazed by her father through the
thick forest that stood between the old Wayne
road and what is now the pike in Wyoming.
She speaks of her teacher being "cruel and
one who whipped hard," but adds, "he never
whipped me." This venerable lady attended
the meeting at the residence of Col. Reily
when Wyoming was selected as the name of
the village, and heard Col. R. express his
preference for that name as it had *seven* letters
in it.

She has seen Indians pass up and down the
very road upon which her quiet home now
stands, seen old Capt. Jacob White, the foremost pioneer of this valley and the block-
houses that stood in this now peaceful valley;
seen many a pioneer laid away in the now neg-
lected grave-yard; heard many a sermon, song
and prayer in meeting houses long since torn
down; seen the old log school house up the
pike developed into the new and costly building just erected in Wyoming; seen the old forest trees fall one by one around her, field after
field cleared, road after road laid out, house
after house built, church spire after church
spire rise. She seems to stand alone—as one
left behind in the march of humanity, as one

who would join the " innumerable caravan "
that has passed on to " God's great town in
the unknown land," leaving her standing amid
kind neighbors and friends, but as one taking
no part and but little interest in the great drama
of human life, upon whose stage she claims to
lag as a superfluous player. May every falter-
ing step be guarded until the sable curtain
shall fall upon the

> " Last scene of all
> That ends this strange, eventful history."

COLONEL ROBERT REILY.

A historical reference to Wyoming at once
suggests this name. Indeed it connects the
annals of this village with the history of our
country. Wyoming and Chancellorsville are
thus associated in the minds of many now
living, as they will be in the memory of succeeding generations. Who was Robert Reily?
He was the youngest son of Mr. John Reily,
born June 1, 1820. It was almost distinction
enough to have had such a father—a Revolutionary soldier and a pioneer of this valley!
He entered the Continental army at the age
of seventeen, and after eighteen months of
valorous service leaving the army, bearing an

honorable discharge, over the hand and seal of General Washington.

He adventured to Kentucky at the age of twenty-one, and in December, 1789, came to the locality now occupied by Carthage, being subsequently driven therefrom by the Indians. He died June 7, 1850, at his home in Hamilton. He was a member of the convention that formed the first constitution of Ohio. The following resolution was passed by the convention assembled at Columbus to revise the constitution of 1802, in session at the time of his death.

Resolved, "That this convention has heard with deep sensibility the announcement of the death of John Reily, Esq., late of the county of Butler, a soldier of the Revolution, one of the early pioneers of the West, one who filled important trusts under the territorial government, and one of the framers of the present constitutions of Ohio."*

Thus was Col. Reily's blood " fetched from fathers of war-proof;" and it is not strange that when the war for the Union broke out, he should be among the bravest to fight, and the noblest to fall, in his country's defense.

---

*McBride's Pioneer Biography.

He assisted Col. N. C. McLean in recruiting the celebrated 75th Ohio Infantry, and at its organization was commissioned major. He fought his first battle at Monterey Court House, in Western Virginia, April 12, 1862. His soldiery bearing and ability brought him into notice at once. At Cedar Mountain he was in the thickest of the fight, also at Graveton, near the field of Bull Run. August 30, 1862, he was promoted to lieutenant-colonel, and January, 1863, was made colonel; and closed his brief but glorious career at Chancellorsville, where he was mortally wounded and died May 5, 1863.

> " Oh ! there was mourning when ye fell,
> In your own vales a deep-toned knell,
> An agony, a wild farewell :—
> Rest with your still and solemn fame ;
> The hills keep record of your name,
> And never can a touch of shame
> Darken the buried brow."

THE PRESBYTERIAN CHURCH

Stands upon a large lot, amply shaded and carpeted with living green, upon the north-west corner of Burns and Wyoming avenues.

It represents an expenditure on the part of

the community of nearly $12,000 in an endeavor to conserve their highest and best interests, and is an index to the high moral and Christian character of this village.

Its location has yet a reservation or removal from the residences clustered about it, and the secular confusions that indicate the rapid march of humanity past it and onward into that future of which its spire and deep-toned bell seem ever to forewarn it.

This church marks an important stage in the religious growth of this valley.

From a historical discourse delivered July, 2, 1876,* we gather some facts relating to its origin.

A Presbyterian church was first organized in Reading, August 29, 1823. Rev. Benjamin Graves was it first minister.

Lockland was then beginning its career as a village.

April 6, 1850, was the natal day of the Lockland Presbyterian church, an outgrowth of the Reading church. The union of the old and new School churches, in 1870, greatly enlarged the Lockland church congregation. About the same time the Rev. Silas Hawley (who had been pastor of the church from

---

* By the Rev. W. A. Hutchinson, late pastor of the Lockland church.

1866) was dismissed with sixty-one members
to form the Presbyterian church at Wyoming.
There are about one hundred and twenty-five
members enrolled at present. The Rev. W.
W. Houston is pastor in charge.

> "'Farewell! farewell! base world, farewell!'
> In touching tones exclaimed a bell;
> 'Life is a boon to mortals given,
> To fit the soul for bliss in heaven;
> Do not invoke th' avenging rod,
> Come here and learn the way to God;
> Say to the world, Farewell! farewell!'
> Pealed forth the Presbyterian bell."

EARLY SCHOOLS.*

"We find that in this immediate neighborhood
were also two of the early schools, one on
Huntsman's place and another on the Paddack
road. Of this last school we have obtained
some valuable and interesting information. In
the days of sixty-five years ago, it was kept by
an aged female, named Betsy Chase. It was
a log-house, heated by an immense fire-place,
with a hole knocked out of one side for a window, which hole was in winter time covered
with a greased paper to keep out the cold, but
to admit the light. Long before the days of
public free schools, it was supported by a tui-

* From Mayor Bromwell's Anniversary address.

tion at so much a quarter; and the teacher probably boarded from house to house, and took part pay in country produce."

THE SCHOOL BUILDING,

Just completed this year, cost about $20,000, and is the largest and most commodious in our valley. It is a shining exponent of the intelligence of this community, and of the progress of our people generally in perfecting our school system. This is the growth from seed sown seventy-five years ago (1807), when Mrs. Wilmuth learned to spell in the old log school-house up the pike.

We may not name all who have nurtured this seed to its apparent maturity and fruit-bearing; but there are names which will always be associated with its culture — Edward P. Allen, Alexander Mayhew, John Martin, John H. Tangeman, Caleb B. Evans, and George S. Stearns were so much identified with its rise and growth as to be deserving of especial mention in this connection.

It stands upon a lot, of three acres, facing north on Wyoming and south on Worthington avenues, and is the costliest temple dedicated to learning in Mill Creek valley; and, in this respect, has its counterpart in the Wayne Avenue church, the costliest of its kind, and, virtually situated between the same avenues, and distant from each other less than one-half mile.

These two splendid structures constitute the high water-mark of religious and educational interests in point of expenditure in construction in our valley.

The present attendance is about two hundred scholars. The popularity of this school and its thorough efficiency is due to the superintendence of Prof. Chas. S. Fay, who for the last eight years has had charge.

In this valley, the days of the perambulatory school teacher are fast passing away—the days when he used to *board around*, whose experience elicited such expressions of sympathy from Mark Twain as the following :

" But there is one man in this world to whom I alwuz take oph my hat, and remain uncovered until he gets safely by, and that is the distrikt skoolmaster.

When I meet him I look upon him az a martyr just returning from the stake, or on his way there tew be cooked.

A distrikt skoolmaster, who duz a square job, and takes his codfish bawls reverently, iz a better man to-day, tew hav lieing around loose, than Solomon would be, arrayed in all ov hiz glory.

Solomon wuz better at writing proverbs and managing a large family than he would be tew navigate a distrikt skoolhous.

Enny man who has kept a distrikt skool for ten years, and boarded around the naberhood, ought to be made a mager gineral and have a penshun for the rest ov his nat'ral days, and a hoss and waggin tew do his going around in."

THE DEPOT.

As a railroad village, Wyoming has risen rapidly in importance. It is at present the northern terminus of the double track from Cincinnati on the C. H. & D. Railroad.

One of the most commodious depots on the road is here located.

A beautiful park is built around it. Mr. Josiah Dwight is the agent in charge.

LANDMARKS.

One of the relics of the Riddle farm was standing only a few years ago in the shape of a log-house on the front of the lot now owned by Dr. Taylor, and the old well and three evergreen trees near his front fence still mark the site of the former building.

On the corner, west of the pike, and next to Mr. Baldwin's, years ago stood an old tannery; but the only evidence of the industry once carried on there is found in the two wells still existing upon the lot.

A log-house was standing there when Mr. Woodruff bought this property, in 1864, which was soon after disposed of by Mr. W. to Jerry Meyers, who transferred it to Greenwood, where it still subserves the purposes of a home.

THE HOMES OF WYOMING.

"The stately homes of England,
  How beautiful they stand!
Amidst their tall ancestral trees,
  O'er all the pleasant land."
                              —*Mrs. Hemans.*

These words will apply with peculiar emphasis and propriety to this wealthy and flourishing suburb.

As a retreat from yonder city, it affords pre-eminent advantages, and is a distinguished instance of the rapid and wonderful growth of this valley.

Elsewhere we have mentioned the homes of Mr. John Carlisle, Mr. E. P. Stout, and Mr.

George S. Stearns—all situated in this village. We here allude to a few more residences for the purpose of further illustrating its development.

THE FRIEND HOMESTEAD

Is the central landmark of Wyoming. Widow Evatt first built a log cabin upon this site in 1814. Isaac B. Riddle, subsequently acquiring title to this and the adjoining ground known as the Riddle farm, tore down the cabin and built a brick house in its stead. This was in 1832. Col. C. W. Friend, then fifteen years old, helped make the brick out of which it was built. The orchard around it, fruitful and abounding with shade, was planted by Mr. Riddle. In 1858 Col. Friend bought eighteen acres, including this house, of Mr. Riddle; subsequently enlarged it and made it his homestead, where he lived until his death. It has an antiquated look, suggesting repose and comfort within its thick-built and venerable walls.

The old well, dug by Mrs. Evatt in 1814, is still there, affording an exhaustless supply of sparkling cold water.

This homestead now belongs to Miss Nettie M., youngest daughter of the late Col. Friend.

THE EVANS MANSION

Is an emblematic country seat. It comprises about eight acres—a superb little manor constituting the cultivated home of MR. AND MRS. C. B. EVANS.

It is a splendid gothic structure, facing east, and from its proud summit looks down, almost disdainfully, upon the valley beneath.

A magnificent panorama is spread out before you as you stand upon its vine-covered porches; and as you contemplate this landscape, painted by the oldest of masters, you will recall the words of Madame Michilet:—

" Nature is immovable and yet mobile. That is her eternal charm. Her unwearied activity, her ever-shifting phantasmagoria do not weary, do not disturb; the harmonious motion bears in itself a profound repose."

THE BARNEY RESIDENCE.

One September day the writer stood on the broad steps that lead up to the home of MR. AND MRS. R. D. BARNEY. The elevated site, the superb structure, the natural scenery, recalled at once the site of Macbeth's castle in the highlands of Scotland :—

DUNCAN.—This castle has a pleasant seat,
          The air nimbly and sweetly recommends itself
          Unto your gentle senses.
BANQUO.—This guest of summer,
          The temple-haunting martlet, does approve,
          By his loved mansionry, that the heaven's breath
          Smells wooingly here: no jutty, frieze, buttress,
          Nor coigne of vantage, but this bird hath made
          His pendant bed and procreant cradle,—
          Where they do haunt, I have observed,
          The air most delicate.

Mr. Barney and his brother Howard, are sons of the late Hon. H. H. Barney, who was long identified with the public school system of Ohio, at one time being State School Commissioner.

They are also members of the great publishing house of Robert Clarke & Co., and as such, should be classed with the younger literary pioneers of this valley.

THE ANDREWS HOMESTEAD

Stands in the midst of a sixty-acre tract, on an eminence shaded by old forest trees. This frame building was *raised* on the afternoon of March 4th, 1861, the contractor deferring the work until the afternoon of that day in order that it might not occur during the Buchanan administration, but rather signalize the incoming of President Lincoln's.

It is worth the while to climb that hill, and then look from its summit up into the clear, pure air, and then away to the cloud-canopied city in the distance.

The home stands upon a point projecting from the ridge of hills, of which it is a part, into the valley. It thus affords a most advantageous view of the valley. The cars on the C. H. & D. can be seen from the time they leave the depot in Glendale until they pass Longview, six miles south. All the villages of the plain may be seen. Away to the south-east rises the Cincinnati Observatory. Numberless church-spires, school-houses, depots, and public institutions are features of this living landscape.

The Dayton Short Line trains may also be seen passing through Sharon and Lockland.

Upon the lot near the house is the stump of what was, doubtless, the largest and the oldest oak in the valley. It now measures eighteen feet and two inches in circumference. Mr. Andrew Harris, from whom the farm was purchased, said that one thousand rails and eleven cords of wood were made out of this tree when it was cut down.

Near it is the tall stump of a remarkably

large mulberry tree, covered with vines, which were planted at the suggestion of Colonel Reily, a school-mate of Mr. Andrews, and his warm, personal friend until his death.

With Mr. and Mrs. Andrews, in this quiet home, still lives the venerable widow of Wm. E. White. She was born in Hartford City, Conn., March 3, 1791. Her father was an officer in the Revolution. She came to Cincinnati, with her husband, in 1818, in a carriage, all the way from Newark, New Jersey. More than four score years and ten have passed over her venerable head, and during that time she has lived under all the Presidents of the Republic.

Mr. and Mrs. White came to Wyoming in 1861, at which time he built this residence. In October, 1870, a meeting was held in this house, upon the invitation of Mr. and Mrs. White, at which the building of a church for "The Wyoming Society of the New Church" was proposed by Mr. White. There were present:

> Mr. and Mrs. R. H. Andrews,
> Mr. and Mrs. S. S. Carpenter,
> Mr. and Mrs. Wm. Leuthstrom,
> Mr. and Mrs. John H. Carter,
> Mr. and Mrs. C. B. Chase,

Mr. and Mrs. E. H. Cowing,
Mr. and Mrs. Theodore Edson.
The enterprise was determined upon. Mr.
White and Mr. Andrews being the largest con-
tributors. The church was completed at a
cost, including lot, of $5,000, December 9th,
1871. Mr. White was buried from that church
just twenty days afterwards.

THE HINSDALE RESIDENCE

On Burns Avenue, stands on a gentle eminence which has been subjected to the
touch of the landscape gardner, but still retaining so many natural characteristics, as to be
seemingly unadorned save by the hand of nature. Studied art would hardly group the
three ashes as they stand out upon the lawn;
and yet because they were thus planted by the
wayward wind in wafting the seed, they have
a special value and an artless, inimitable beauty.
So all the shrubbery is of nature's planting,
excepting a scarlet maple here and there, the
wild-tulip, and other select shrubbery.

Its exterior is in marked contrast with the
many beautiful residences around it. It is a
departure in architecture. Say rather that it
is a *renaissance* of an antique art fallen into

desuetude only because of its costliness. It can not be described. Wide steps lead up to an enclosed piazza, canopied with an artistic roof, whose ceilings are paneled and oiled white walnut. Above this is a hooded *loggia*, suggesting a resemblance between this and the house of Capulet, in Verona, and that some time a future Juliet, leaning therefrom in the moonlight, might sigh and say, " O Romeo, Romeo, wherefore art thou Romeo?" He who designed this odd, angular, superb home must have put himself into " the trick of singularity."

The colors upon the house are dark green mellowing to old gold, and warmed here and there with *couleur de rose*.

This is the residence of MR. AND MRS. LORING HINSDALE.

PROF. G. A. CARNAHAN'S

Grandfather, James Carnahan, was born in the year 1777, in Pennsylvania, and came to Ohio in 1797.

In the first directory of Cincinnati (1819), we learn that James Carnahan and Joseph Cilley were the first two Justices of the Peace appointed for Colerain township.

William Carnahan (father of the professor) was born in this township in 1804, and in 1829 married Miss Maria L. Davis, of Warren county. These venerable pioneers are still living at New Burlington.

Thus it appears that for eighty-five years the Carnahans have been pioneers and citizens of Springfield township.

Professor Carnahan, himself a pioneer in educational matters, and at present Principal of the First Intermediate School of Cincinnati, lives in a pleasant, refined home of his own on Beech Avenue.

MR. GRANT H. BURROWS'

Residence, on Elm and Walnut avenues, will always attract attention as a home that was not built without much study being given to its plan. Probably no house in the valley was more carefully and thoughtfully devised, as a home for wife and children, than this. It stands almost in the center of the old Burns farm, which owes its marvelously sudden transformation into a village to the business generalship of the gentleman who now resides in this splendid suburban home.

But the view from the *belvedere* is so far and so fine, that we must try to portray it in a ver-

bal way. So we enter the open door, mount
the grand stairway, glancing at the highly-
finished woodwork, the costly, mirror-like mantels, look through the invisible plate-glass windows, then up another stairway to the *belvedere*.
It is morning. The sun has not altogether dis-
pelled the blended smoke and vapor that float
like billows over the valley and envelope
the hills. But in every direction you see
towers, and spires, and domes rising from the
bosom of that imaginary sea. Seeing this, it
is but natural to indulge in the illusion that you
are passing the Dardanelles on board an
English merchantman, and that what you see
far away to the south are the mosques and minarets of the old Byzantium capital, rising above
the sea of Marmora.

THE PALMER RESIDENCE

Was recently built by G. G. Palmer, Esq.,
It is a substantial, commodious, and imposing
structure, beautiful in design within and without,
and stands on a large elevated lot on the north-
east corner of Burns Avenue and Park place.
A well-kept lawn spreads away from the
house in every direction, and many old forest trees surround it. Nothing, seemingly,
has been omitted in the construction and fur-

nishment of this house, that would conduce to its being both a perpetual and delightful home.

"Therefore, when we build, let us think that we build forever. Let it not be for present delight, nor for present uses alone; let it be such a work as our descendants will thank us for, and let us think, as we lay stone upon stone, that a time is to come when those stones will be held sacred because our hands have touched them."

CHARLES H. VAUGHAN, ESQ.,

Resides in a beautiful home on Worthington Avenue, next west of the school building.

These buildings, standing where they do, strikingly illustrate the extent to which reclamation of this valley has been carried in particular localities; for there was once here a lake, peculiar to this then forest-shaded soil, upon which many a wild duck has been shot by the pioneers of Wyoming.

The dream of a rural home must be fully realized in possessing this tasteful and commanding residence.

HON. JUDGE HARMON

Lives in a retired and comfortable home, also on Worthington Avenue. The lot upon which

his residence stands was doubtless the margin
of the Woodland lake, elsewhere described.

"Friends, books, a garden, and perhaps his pen,
Delightful industry enjoyed at home,
And nature, in her cultivated trim,
Dressed to his taste."

PROF. JACOB H. BROMWELL,

At present Mayor of the village, resides on
Mt. Pleasant Avenue. This is a model country
home, the repository of many books, and the
scene of constant mental and moral culture.
In this way the professor is paying tribute to
the widening stream of civilization that finds
an ever-deepening channel in this valley.

MR. GEORGE HOUSE

Possesses a representative residence in this
village, situated on the south-east corner
of Burns and Wyoming avenues. Old oaks
and elms shadow the lawn and make an artificial twilight even at noonday.

"The elm trees stirless in the unbreathing calm,
And all the lush-red roses drooped in dream—"

Is a characteristic of this home scene on many
a mid-summer evening.

DR. C. P. HART'S RESIDENCE.

This is a tasteful structure, with tower, porches, bay windows, &c., on the corner of Burns and Worthington avenues. The Doctor's unique little office, in the corner of the lot, is a professional adjunct to the same, the whole attracting notice from the railroad.

REUBEN TYLER, ESQ.,

At one time Mayor, and at present Solicitor of the village, resides in a pleasant home of his own construction on Burns Avenue. It stands upon a knoll overlooking Maplewood and Hartwell, and amid the trees that stood there when it was a part of the section originally purchased by Mahlon Ford, Esq., and subsequently the farm of Archibald Burns, from whom this popular avenue derives its name.

THE RANSOM RESIDENCE,

Situated in the bend of Elm Avenue, is a conspicuous instance in point, showing the improvement that has taken place on the Burns farm since it was owned by Archibald Burns, Esq. It is a commodious and substantial frame, facing the north star, and surmounted by an observatory affording entrancing views in all directions, and upon which rises still higher a flagstaff, from which, when unfolded, our banner of beauty and glory may be seen from Glendale to Clifton heights. This is the home of COLONEL AND MRS. E. P. RANSOM.

THE STORY OF THE FLAG,

That now and then floats so proudly above the home of Colonel Ransom, may be gathered from the following military order:

HEAD-QUARTERS 1ST BRIG., 2D DIV. }
Camp Ella Bishop. }

Lexington, Ky., October 28, 1862.

GENERAL ORDER No. 2:

When the rebels occupied this portion of the State, they treated with disrespect all evidences of loyalty, and heaped their insults upon citizens by hauling from the steeples and windows of their houses the emblem of their liberty and nationality, the flag of our armies, the ensign of our Republican institutions, and the banner we are so willing to defend; they trailed it in the dust and trampled it under their unhallowed feet, and shouted it should wave no more

over the city of Lexington or the State of Kentucky. But, in the midst of their traitorous
shouts, following in the wake of the trailing
banner, a bold and patriotic, yet beautiful and
modest young lady, scarcely eighteen years of
age, one of Kentucky's proudest daughters,
rushed forth with wounded spirit, yet undaunted
courage, rescued it from the traitor's grasp, with-
stood their threats, and waved it above her head.

She rescued it—she waved it—she saved it,
and to-day holds it, proudly protected by the
gallant soldiers from Illinois, Michigan, and
Ohio.

As an humble evidence, therefore, of respect
and admiration for such patriotism and worthy
example, this camp shall bear the name of that
young lady—ELLA BISHOP.

By command of

BRIG.-GEN. G. CLAY SMITH.

GREEN CLAY GOODLOE,

Lieut., and Aid-de-Camp.

This thrilling incident reached the ear of an
officer then serving upon the staff of General
Smith. One year afterwards they were married; but this then famous lady lost none of
her distinction in becoming MRS. COL. RANSOM.

The flag was a wedding present from Mrs. Frank Fitch, who made it with her own loyal hands, and to whom it belonged when rescued from the rebels by Miss Ella Bishop.

CHAPTER XVIII.

GEORGE GEORGE, ESQ.,

ONE of the pioneers of this valley, at present one of the Justices of the Peace in Springfield township, is now a resident of this village, having built several houses. His home is an elegant brick, facing west on Elm Avenue.

MR. CHARLES S. WOODRUFF,

One of the oldest residents of this suburb, and one that has done much by way of building and otherwise improving his property, to enlarge and beautify Wyoming, resides in his own comfortable home on the pike. This is a large, well-kept and imposing homestead, and almost in the exact center of the village.

Mr. Woodruff purchased this property and built this house during the last war, and as having taken a conspicuous part in developing this village, deserves to be classified as one of its oldest pioneers.

JOHN H. TANGEMAN, ESQ.

Perhaps no gentleman has taken a livelier interest in Wyoming, or is animated by village pride to a greater extent than Mr. Tangeman. While not perhaps contributing so much to its up-building as a Burrows, a Stearns, or a Woodruff (his business interests being chiefly in Lockland), yet such has been his sympathy for schools and churches and all benevolent enterprises that, in this regard, he rises in importance as one of its foremost residents. Moreover, he is a pioneer in its strict sense; and many are the incidents he can tell touching the early settlement of this community.

He is the projector of the Baptist Church enterprise, which contemplates the erection of a place of worship in this village soon.

WILLIAM H. CARRUTHERS, ESQ.

This gentlemen owns a delightful homestead about which historical associations are beginning to cluster. It was one of the first residences built in the village, and was first occupied by Mr. John C. Thorpe, now a resident of the East. It then (1860) passed into the hands of General Jacob Ammen, who was a distinguished officer in the late war.

JAMES K. HURIN, ESQ.,

Has greatly contributed to the improvement of the village in remodeling the old Leuthstrom property and converting it into his homestead. It occupies a prominent location on the corner of Reily and Glendale avenues, and, together with his grounds, is a noble type of suburban residence. Many beautiful old trees, and a choice selection of flowering shrubs adorn the grounds.

DR. J. Q. A. COFFEEN

Is a native of the Miami valley, having been born, about fifty years ago, near Lebanon. Mrs. Coffeen is a grand-daughter of Wm. Chamberlain, the founder of Springdale—one of the oldest and most respected pioneers of the valley.

The Doctor has a pleasant home on Wyoming Avenue. He is a brother-in-law of Dr. Shepherd, of Glendale, and at one time was in partnership with him.

THE WYOMING IMPROVEMENT COMPANY

Is a voluntary association of gentlemen having in view the æsthetic interests of the village.

Their self-imposed duties consist of tree culture, looking after the parks, planting flowers by the wayside, etc.

They operate under a law paramount to village ordinances—that of eminent domain.

They are doing much in this way to beautify the village; and as it is done at their own expense, it is all the more disinterested and commendable.

Wyoming is a prominent postal station, of which Mr. Charles H. Slack is post-master.

PROMINENT RESIDENTS.

The following is a list of the citizens, not elsewhere mentioned, who have invested their means in building pleasant homes in this village :

Mr. W. H. Sarvis.	Mr. Geo. S. LaRue.
Dr. C. R. Taft.	Mr. Albert Stearns.
Mr. John W. Fox.	Rev. Mr. Sutton.
Prof. W. H. Pabodie.	Mr. E. H. Cowing.
John W. Hill, Esq.	J. F. Jewett, Esq.
Mr. Edw. Mitchell.	Mr. W. DeForrest.
Capt. James F. Merrill.	R. P. Fox, Esq.
Geo. H. Friend, Esq.	Mr. Geo. H. Stearns.
W. F. Colburn, Esq.	Wm. A. Clark, Esq.

Prof. E. H. Pritchard. Mrs. A. Compton.
Mr. John W. Pfaff. Mr. Joseph Humphreys.
Mr. G. W. Hartwell. Mr. John Pollock.
Major Geo. B. Fox. Mr. R. L. Cilley.
Israel H. Pendery, Esq. Mrs. E. D. Bennett.
Dr. Taylor. Maj. W. F. Armstrong.
C. S. Woodruff, Jr. Goodloe Pendery.
Mr. Geo. Miles. Mr. N. Curtis,
Mr. Harry Pollock. H. D. Peck, Esq.
Mr. T. F. George. Orson Britton, Esq.
Mr. Charles Ault. Mr. Schuberth.
Rev. John Haight. Prof. C. B. Chase.
Mr. Walter Baldwin. Mr. Zach. George.
Mr. Weidler. Mr. Ash Baldwin.
Mr. George Stoddart. Mr. Golding.
Mr. Clifford Baldwin. Mr. Charles Mitchell.
Mr. A. C. Tyler. R. B. Moore, Esq.
Mr. Van Zant. Dr. Negley.
Mr. Josiah Dwight. Mr. John Rychen.
Mr. C. B. Maddux.

CHAPTER XIX.

GLENDALE.

IT is the observation of a gentleman* who has traveled much in Europe that the view to the east and north as you enter Glendale from the south on the railroad, presents a striking resemblance to that in Roxburghshire, Scotland, and particularly around Melrose Abbey, " a remarkable monument of antiquites and one of the most distinguished, founded on the banks of the Tweed, and the nursery of learned and religious men."

THE NAME.

The ground upon which it is built being purchased from Mr. E. R. Glenn, his name entered into the compound. The synonymous suffix " dale" was added in order to have a beautiful name ; although it is somewhat misleading to the stranger, the suggestion being

---

*Mr. John Carlisle.

that it is located deep down in a valley, whereas it is a little city set upon a hill beautiful for situation and the pride of the Miami valley.

It has a shrubbery that "Shenstone might have envied," shading all its walks and avenues. Many of its places are enclosed by hedges, and Glendale presents the appearance of an immense park. Already the axe is laid at the root of many a superfluous tree. Its delightful homes have the air of affluence and all that wealth may bring to comfort, refine, and ennoble. Other suburbs may have more elegant residences, but certainly not more elegant residents. Others may not be so far from the city, but, in point of time consumed in reaching them, fully as remote.

THE MOUND BUILDERS

Seemed to have loved this locality, for Glendale is circumvallated with these ancient earth works.

When the Hamilton pike was constructed it cut through a very large mound to the south of the village on the grounds of Mrs. Cummings, near the locality of Station springs. The west half is still discernible. Large skeletons were found in it when cut through. The next north is the well-known one on Mr. French's farm, three-quarters of a mile distant, between which communication could easily be made.

About half a mile west and north of that is another, on a commanding point projecting into the valley. From this mound a view is obtained to the west up Mill creek for five miles to a point on the hills opposite, and to the south almost the entire length of the valley. North of this is another on the land now owned by Mr. John H. Porter. This is now quite small ; but north of this, on the land of Mr. C. H. Allen, and not far north and west of the old Hamilton house, are the remains of two remarkable mounds, now almost reduced to a level with the surrounding field.

From these mounds a magnificent view may be obtained in all directions, but especially to the south and north. The smaller mounds above named may all be seen from it, and indeed the whole range of hills immediately above and north of Cincinnati. There can be no doubt but that these mounds are part of a system that extended to, and communicated with, the great mound near the mouth of Mill creek in Cincinnati. There is still another

small one in the grove belonging to Mr. Shoemaker, in the village limits, not far west of the
railroad.

"While standing thus upon thy oak-crowned head,
The shadows of dim ages long since gone
Reel on my mind, like spectres of the dead,
While dirge-like music haunts the wind's low moan.
From out the bosom of the boundless Past
There rises up no voice of thine to tell!
Eternal silence, like a shadow vast,
Broods on thy breast, and shrouds thine annals well."

THE WAYNE WAR TRACE

May be seen by standing at the toll-gate and
looking across to the residence of Henry M.
Skillman, Esq. The general course of this
army, as it descended from the high ground
now occupied by Woodlawn, is denoted by the
present road way. It is difficult to conceive
the fact that this army worked its way through
this locality, covered as it was by a dense,
wild forest. The trees had to be cut down
and cleared away before the troops, and wagons,
and artillery could pass over it.

Glendale, to-day, is a polished monument
to that civilization of which Wayne's
army was the rude forerunner. It is an out-
post of Cincinnati on its march to Hamilton,

being midway between old Fort Washington and old Fort Hamilton.

A LANDMARK.

The Hamilton house, sometimes called the Snodgrass house, still standing upon the farm of Mr. C. H. Allen, immediately west of Glendale near the Springdale pike, is a remarkable monument of past generations. It was built about the year 1807 by Mr. Hamilton, a wealthy gentleman, whose permanent home was in New Orleans, this being intended as a summer residence.

About fifty-five years ago it was a tavern stand, and kept by Mr. Thomas Drake. It passed to Major Joseph Harris, who, at one time, owned a large tract west of the pike extending south to, and including, the farm of Mr. Maynard French.

It was a grand house in its day. Time has covered its once fine face with wrinkles. The huge fire-place is there, but a cold and desolate hearth-stone is spread out before it. Its warmth, and cheer, and charm are gone forever.

GRAVE-YARDS.

There is one upon the Skillman farm, a

family burying-ground, in which the ancestors
of Mr. Henry M. Skillman sleep. Another
was near the present site of the public school
building adjoining the old log church in which
the Rev. Warwick preached seventy-five
years ago. Another is on the farm of Mr. W. A. Proc-
ter in the edge of the woods near the eastern
corporation line of the village. About this
latter place there is almost an appalling mystery.

Every other place of the kind, visited by the
writer in this valley, has some evidences of
Christian burial other than mere rough stones.
But here are probably fifty graves. Time
has rolled them level with the surface of the
earth. Upon those stones, taken from the
adjacent ravine, there is not a name, mark,
sign, or device. "There is no knowledge in
the grave" whither they have gone. That
this was a burying-ground for a savage race
there is but little doubt; but whether they
were laid there with tears of sorrow or "with
awful laughter" we may never know. This
we do know: "One generation passeth away
and another generation cometh, but the earth
abideth forever."

Standing upon these places where our pre-

decessors have paused to put aside their dead,
and then marched on into the shadowy future,
the words of Elizabeth Stuart Phelps come
to mind :

" Let us endure, enjoy, strive, sing, bleed,
smile, aspire, and go to our graves gratefully.
Over our dumb and witless ashes a select and
proud race, with the beauty of the pagan gods,
shall walk haughtily, and with the scorn of the
gods shall remember us as we remember the
savage, whose war shouts assisted in developing the fine human larynx to contribute to
the modulations of the voice Malibran."

OLD TAVERNS.

The first tavern stood west of the toll-gate.
It was kept by Andrew Van Dyke, a son-in-
law of Major Joseph Harris, about 1812. A
Mr. Heffner kept it for a while. He died there.
His widow then built a brick tavern where
Mrs. Samuel B. Allen's stone residence stands.

These public houses stood at the conjunction
of the old and new Hamilton roads, and were
the scenes of busy times in early days.

Mr. Henry M. Skillman recollects the old
stage passengers walking up the hill through
his father's farm, and seeing thousands of hogs
driven over the same road.

Another remarkable scene was the trains of market wagons ; twenty to fifty at a time, with seldom less than six horses to a team, and each of those proud horses wearing bells, the sound of which seemed to please them, from the fact that, while standing, they would keep tossing their heads to make the bells ring.

Mr. Richard W. Keys, now a resident of Glendale, passed over this road in 1831 in one of those old stages. He started from his home in Cincinnati at daylight, stopped at the old tavern, and arrived at Oxford at ten o'clock at night. Many illustrious men have passed over this road from Cincinnati to Hamilton, especially the leading lawyers of the city, to attend the courts at Hamilton ; among these may be mentioned Hon. William Corry, Hon. W. S. Groesbeck, and Judge Burnet. It is related of the two former that the stage upset once in crossing Mill creek below Foster's hill, and, that getting thoroughly wet, they stopped at Spillman's tavern to dry their clothes and *warm* themselves.

"THE LAST OF THE BARONS."

Many a year ago, 1807, Rev. Robert War-wick owned the ground upon which the prin-

cipal part of Glendale now stands. He was a
minister of "The Reformed Dissenting Presbyterian Congregation." He was of Scotch-
Irish extraction, and a remarkable man in his
way, and accounted a good one. His rude
home stood where Mr. William B. Keys now
lives. At first he preached in a log meeting-
house that stood about where the public school
building is located. It was subsequently supplanted by a frame building, about thirty feet
square, with a high roof and a platform somewhat raised and built especially for his use.
He walked up and down the stage while
preaching, spoke very deliberately; would
preach seldom less than four hours at a time,
and sometimes all day. The singing was remarkably fine for those days. His daughter
Eleanor would sit upon the platform with her
father and line the hymns for him. No hymn
books were used, the daughter reading each
line, and so reading it that the tones of her
voice began and ended in the seemingly uninterrupted song. Old residents remember
its effect, even though over seventy years
have elapsed since they heard it.

It is said of this pioneer preacher that, during his prolonged sermons, he would recuper-
ate his failing physical forces by pausing, now

and then, to drink butter milk from a jug that
stood conveniently at hand.   It was a saying
of his " that he could drink the buttermilk of
seven cows, and that sometimes he borrowed
from his neighbors."

His congregation were called " Warwick-
ites." He was regarded as an educated man,
for his day, was a leader of the people, owned
considerable property, had many followers,
and after several years of labor in the locality,
he removed to Piqua, where he died after one
day's sickness.   He was evidently a man of
great force of character, and could, if necessary,
say as authoritatively as the old Earl of Warwick :

> " The proudest he that holds up Lancaster
> Dares not stir a wing if Warwick shake his bells."

MRS. LOUISA SEWARD CUMMINGS.

This venerable lady is the daughter of Mr.
James Seward, mentioned on page 44 in connection with Pleasant Valley Station.   He was
one of the earliest settlers in this vicinity, and
derived his title to his half section directly
from John Cleves Symmes, the deed being still
in possession of his daughter.   This property
is located immediately south of the Maynard

French farm. Mrs. Cummings lives in a little frame house, standing back a short distance from the pike, on a bluff overlooking Mill creek. She was born upon this farm March 4, 1809, in a log-house which stood where Mr. William Riddle now lives, across the creek, and has never lived anywhere else.

Her father was killed by a falling tree in 1817, while procuring timber for the purpose of building a better house. He was laid out in that unfinished house, which since has been converted into a barn by Mr. Riddle, and may be seen from the pike, not much resembling a house nor looking altogether unlike a barn.

In 1832 she married Mr. Joseph Cummings, whom she survives.

Her recollection of early and later events is remarkable, and her narration of them interesting and intelligent.

From her we gather much of the information submitted relative to the old landmarks about Glendale. She remembers the Warwicks, the Harris family, the elder Riddles, the Van Dykes, the Hamiltons, the Spillmans, and the Fosters.

Her father was probably the first capitalist who engaged in the business of house-building, in this vicinity at least. As a bachelor, he built four log cabins on his farm in succession, selling them to the early settlers as they would arrive. He finally married one of the daughters of a Jerseyman to whom he had sold, and thereupon built a cabin for himself.

Mrs. Cummings remembers particularly one *stylish* family, as she terms it, named So-field, for whom he built a log cabin out of hewed ash logs, with ash boards for flooring, and a brick chimney inside. This was regarded as quite a fine house at that day. Ten years ago this Mrs. Sofield, then being 105 years old, was in Washington applying for a pension on the ground that her husband was a soldier in the war of 1812.

This cabin stood beside the old Mill creek road, which pursued a course a little west of where the pike is now.

The days of her pilgrimage are more than three-score years and ten.

"When even at last the solemn hour shall come," may it be but the fleeting, painless shadow, that foretells eternal sunshine beyond the cloudland of this life.

THE SKILLMAN FARM,

Adjoining Glendale immediately on the south, and extending originally from the pike

eastwardly one mile, being from section line
to section line, is a patrimony of which the
present inheritor may justly be proud.

This is a remarkable estate in a land characterized by mutations of title, in a land of sub-
division, mortgages, and leaseholds. From
the United States, through Symmes, to Jacob
Skillman in 1805, then by descent to Abraham,
and upon his death, to Henry M. Skillman, the
present owner, is a brief abstract of the title to
this noted estate by freehold.

This farm now consists of 275 acres, in a
highly-improved condition, rich in soil, beautiful as to contour, with all the out-buildings;
machinery, etc., necessary to its cultivation,
and not an acre of waste land upon it. When
his grandfather came and located this ground,
it was a magnificent woodland realm, consisting of oak, walnut, ash, and sugar trees. For
centuries some of them had waited for the
coming of that hardy race from the denuded
hills and valleys of the old Jersey State.

The first house built was that still standing
upon the hill side, old and decayed, but in its
day called the "White House," so attractive
was it and so well finished. It was built in
1806, of hewed logs at first, and subsequently
weather boarded. The next house constructed was that in which Mr. Skillman now lives,

about a year or so after the first. It was the eastern portion of the house, and to which Mr. S. has made large additions. Here he was born in 1824.

There was a time in the history of this farm when a man could walk upon fallen timber from the east to the west line. A large sugar camp stood next to the site of Glendale in which maple sugar and molasses have been made in great quantities.

This farm has risen out of the past as if touched by the magical wand of Prospero.

Mr. S. walks about it as if every spot were endeared by associations, every acre telling a pathetic story of hardships endured by his fore-fathers in clearing, tilling, and enriching, partly for their self-support, and partly for those who should come after them.

And this farm belongs to the domain of general history. Forty feet to the west of the spot where the homestead stands, passed Wayne's army, the trace of which, as it felled the trees and forced its way through the farm, may be distinctly seen.

Mr. Skillman married a daughter of Judge Luke Foster, and they were married upon Foster's hill. Since which time they have journeyed together in peace and prosperity until wealth is enjoyed without a display of it, while they are surrounded by many friends of early and later years.

"CASTLE WARWICK."

The Rev. Robert Warwick once lived in a hewed log-house on the site now occupied by the residence of Mr. and Mrs. Wm. B. Keys. This was about the year 1807. Some time afterwards it was enlarged by Warwick into a pretentious frame, about forty feet long and twenty feet wide, which was the envy of the neighborhood. When, however, his envious neighbors entered into the house they were somewhat reconciled to the disparity as to houses, for it was very scantily furnished.

This property subsequently passed to Mr. James Glenn, who supplanted the frame in part by a brick structure; the two, combined, formed one house for awhile. It subsequently passed to Mr. Edmund R. Glenn, who again enlarged it by the addition of the brick dwelling which stood there at the time Glendale was laid out. At the first sale of lots in Glendale, Mr. Anthony Harkness acquired title to the Glenn homestead.

Mr. Keys married Miss Emma Harkness, a

granddaughter to Mr. Harkness, a gentleman distinguished for his great wealth and as being of the earliest and largest property holders in the village. Upon his death, Miss Harkness became the owner of the Glenn homestead. After a tour through Europe, Mr. and Mrs. Keys determined to remodel the old landmark again.

This was done by adopting its plan and enlarging upon it. Part of the material of the old was thus incorporated into the new structure, and the old house thereby maintained its identity as well as locality. This house now represents an investment of about $12,000— a development from the "lodge in a vast wilderness," that amounts to a convincing argument in favor of the doctrine of evolution even in the matter of house building.

It is built of brick in the Queen Anne style. Its exterior is almost indescribable, save that it is just like any other house, but that it is like all other houses.

Its red tile roof is its most distinguishable feature, rendering it the first object seen in Glendale at a distance ; and appropriately does it deserve this conspicuousness, as it is the most illustrious landmark in the village.

Its interior is imposing. Three pairs of

folding doors, when open, convert it into one spacious room. From its hooded balcony in the fourth story a magnificent view to the east may be obtained; and when unfurled from that towering staff, his flag may be seen "from thence to Inverness," and as if floating above the walls of some beautiful castle.

"HARWOOD PLACE,"

Consisting of 120 acres, just south of Glendale, derives its name from the late Edward Harwood, and is the home of MR. AND MRS. MAYNARD FRENCH.

The highly-cultivated condition of this property gives it a representative character, and as an illustration of the development of farming interests in this fertile valley, mention of it is here made.

Mr. Harwood is well remembered as an energetic, honorable business man, an old resident of the city and valley, and as one of the strongest opponents of slavery before the red hand of war abolished it. As such he befriended many a poor slave in his efforts to gain his freedom, to obtain which, he then had to flee to Canada, *across the State of Ohio.*

This he did at the peril of his life and property. But such were his convictions, and he

acted accordingly. We see now that all such
opponents of human slavery were simply the
advance of that great army which finally swept
the curse and shame from the land.

The first house on the farm was a frame,
and was built by Major Harris previous to
1829. It burned down about twelve years
ago, whereupon Mr. Marsh built the brick
residence now occupied by Mr. French.

There are ten buildings, exclusive of the
house, upon this place, consisting of a stable
over fifty years old, a new barn, granaries,
carriage-houses, etc. Twenty head of fine cat-
tle, and as many horses, necessitate these out-
buildings. There is a remarkably well-
preserved Indian mound upon this place. Back
of the residence, and down upon the bank of
Mill creek, and on this farm, Major Harris built
a saw mill about 1829. Immediately adjoining
it was a fulling mill. Mr. Wm. Jones, while he
owned the farm, fitted up a carding machine and
a fulling-mill, so that at one and the same
time, a saw-mill, a fulling-mill, and a carding
machine, were in operation upon this farm,
about a half a century ago.

Silence reigns there now. It is a desolate
spot. Imagination alone can give them a
"local habitation and a name."

" The mill wheel clicked, and the mill wheel clacked,
    And the groaning grooves once creaked and cracked,
    And the children came and played,—
    The lazy team, in the days of yore,
    Munched their fodder at the old mill door,
    Or drowsed in the grateful shade.

But the good wife died, and the miller died,
    And the children all went far and wide
    From the play-ground by the dam ;
    But the play-ground now is grass o'ergrown,
    As the mossy foot of the old grave-stone
    Where the old folks sleep so calm."

A LIBRARY.

Mr. Robert Clarke, of the firm of Robert Clarke & Co., resides on Fountain Avenue. The house was originally built at the time Glendale was laid out by Mr. Ezra Elliott, of whom Mr. Clarke purchased. He greatly improved it by the addition of another story, a mansard roof, a wide, deep porch, and in various other respects.

It is one of the most pleasing houses as to its appearance in the village. Its situation is remarkably fine, the lot extending from Fountain Avenue to the Princeton pike in the rear.

THE LIBRARY ROOM

Is an adjunct to the house, specially con-

structed for that purpose. It is twenty-six feet
long and eighteen feet wide, the ceiling rising
to a dome over twenty feet high. The interior is finished with ash and black walnut,
paneled. The walls are doubled, to prevent
dampness from penetrating to the books. They
are covered with book-cases without doors or
glass covers. The bay window is reserved
for plants and flowers. These cases are filled
with rare, old, expensive, and beautiful books;
perhaps the most extensive, and certainly the
best selected, library in the West.

This collection has been the result of forty
years of labor and study, involving a great
outlay of money. Six thousand volumes are
here companionated, comprising two thousand
scientific works; fifteen hundred upon biography; many works upon Scottish history; old
dramatic and literary history of England; and
many a "quaint and curious volume of for-
gotten lore."

The *oldest* book in the library is "Restitu-
tionum Utilissimum," by Francisco De Platea,
printed in Venice in 1478.

The oldest *English* book is "Deversite de
Courtz," printed in Norman French, and published in London 1523, and at one time in the
library of Sir Samuel Romilly.

The *finest* book, " The Poetical Works of Milton," printed by Bulmer for Boydell,—a royal folio, consisting of three large, thick volumes, filled with the most expensive engravings from all editions.

The most *curious* book is the " Nuremberg Chronicle," printed by Koberg in 1493,—a history of the world, profusely illustrated, and in which, for the first time, death is represented as a skeleton.

Here we see a copy of " Locke on the Human Understanding," which belonged to Samuel Johnson, and was in his library, 1723.

A black letter copy of the " Golden Boke of Marcus Aurelius," 1546, presented to Robert Southey, by John Kenzon.

A copy of Ossian's Poems, which belonged to George Washington, and bears his autograph.

No. 29 of The "Weekly News," the first paper published in England, May 2, 1623.

A sermon preached at Hampton Court, by William James, 1578.

Ludolph's Life of Christ, 1474, Prussian Manuscript, on vellum paper, containing the Alcoran in black and red ink, a fine specimen of Eastern calligraphy. Very old.

A Bible printed in Cambridge, 1533. Ritson's Scottish songs, containing autograph of Robert Burns.

"John Ray's Remains," with Sir Walter Scott's autograph.

"Hours of Idleness," the first book printed by George Gordon, Lord Byron, a minor.

"The Chase," the first publication made by by Sir Walter Scott.

"Latin Vulgate Bible," printed at Nuremberg, 1478, by Koberg.

The first edition of "Junius' Letters," 1772.

"English Manuscript," supposed to have been written by Bishop Gilbert Burnet, in 1674, and entitled a "Court Sermon."

"Matthias' Pursuits of Literature," filled with fine portraits, a folio copy.

"*Officium Beatæ Mariæ Virginis,*" an old, rare manuscript, written in silver ink, with four small miniatures, illuminated in gold and colors, old calf, gold tooling, gilt edges, and two clasps, dated 1477.

Among these books one may be at peace, but not alone. They are companions speaking in a "still, small voice" out of the past. Here are the garnered thoughts of centuries. Here may be learned the story of an orphaned Shakspeare, feeding on "adversity's sweet milk," fortune favoring him only after fame

had written that name the highest on the
world's scroll of intellectually great men.
Here may be read the story of the homeless
Homer, the imprisoned Bunyan, the impover-
ished Coleridge, the blind Milton and the
deaf Beethoven ; how that heartless criticism
and

> "Chill penury repressed the noble rage
> And froze the genial current of the soul "

Of the gentle-hearted Keats ; how that the
life of John Huss went out with the flames
that curled around his head as a martyr to
Christianity ; how that Luther inaugurated the
Reformation, and the Mayflower came with
the Pilgrims and left upon our shore,

> "What they there found—
> Freedom to worship God."

These things, and many, many more, are
told you as you turn the pages of these almost
numberless books.

Then wheeling a seat in front of the glowing
grate, the mind runs back to the time when
a nameless ship landed on our shores in 1840,
bringing from Annan, Scotland, a youth of
twelve years of age, seeking his fortune ; and

having found it in a successful business career, found also a beautiful home in Glendale.

To-day this gentleman is the leading publisher in the West. Like snow fall the leaves from his presses. He is the embodiment of this age of printing,

—"lording it o'er
An ever-widening realm of books."

At his home he is among books, and at his store ; on his way to and from his home, books, papers, catalogues, and pamphlets are his companions.

There is no printed catalogue of this library. He needs none. Each book is known by its name and place.

They are his treasure, and there is his heart also, for as yet that busy brain and kind heart have given undivided time and devotion to MINERVA alone.

AN ART MUSEUM.

Mr. Austin Gunnison's residence might be termed "the Art Museum of Glendale." It is a wonderful illustration of the development of this valley in the matter of art culture.

From its porch facing east, affording an entrancing view of natural and artificial scenery, the eye musingly rests upon the remains of a log cabin upon the hill-side within the village limits. It has been but three score years and ten since it was one of the dozen cabins in this vicinity. From that cabin-home to this! Mr. Gunnison's library room was constructed specially to contain his books and his varied and costly art collections. It extends the entire length of the house and adjoins the main building on the east.

This room, and, indeed, the whole house, is the repository of rare, and old, and expensive paintings, statuary, books, and relics, gathered from foreign lands and selected with experienced judgment and consummate taste, of which the following are but a few selections :

"Monte Cavo," near Rome, painted by *Dwight Benton*, at one time a resident of Mill Creek Valley.

"Mercury," in Serpentine marble, from Florence.

"Norwegian Scenery," by *Hans Gude*.

"Siege of Troy," cut in Parian marble.

"The Duke of Brabant," an old placque.

"Achilles' Armor."

"The Dance of the Bears," by Beard.

"Leg of an Old Roman Chair," in marble.

"An old Scottish Banner."

"Austrian Tyrol," by Webber.

"Old Italian Pottery," date 1648.

"Venetian Door-knocker," from a palace on the Grand Canal in Venice.

"A collection of Faces in marble," exhumed from the ruins of Pompeii.

"A pair of old Gauntlets," which have seen service in the days of Knight-Errantry.

"Old English Oak," taken from Trinity Church, Statford-upon-the-Avon, and fashioned into mantel ornaments.

"Old English carving," also part of the mantel.

"Puck," original marble statute, by Harnish.

"A Very Old Painting," by *Van Ostade*.

"Hawking," by Wouverman.

"Ootenbogardus," by Rembrandt.

"A desk of Ebony and Ivory," from Milan.

"Mythological Vases," from Cyprus and Catacombs.

"Old Pottery Furnace," 1548.

"Old Faces in Marble," exhumed in Rome.

"An old Dutch Carving," representing the extent and power of Dutch commerce.

"Ashen Urn," from Catacombs of Rome, used to contain ashes after cremation.

"Venetian Hall Chair."

"An old English clock."

"Pan," an old marble statue ; very curious.

" The Forum Romanum," under which Scientists are now exploring.

" A Japanese Card Basket," with portraits of Marie Antoinette and others; time of Louis XVI.

Mr. Gunnison has a private library of about fifteen hundred volumes ; many of his books being collected while abroad.

MR. SAMUEL J. THOMPSON,

Of the distinguished law firm of King, Thompson & Maxwell, has been a resident of this village for nearly thirty years.

Justice Stanley Matthews and Mr. Thompson lived next door to each other on Longworth street in the city, and as neighbors determined at the same time to make Glendale their future home, and accordingly moved out the same Summer. Mr. Thompson, as a professional gentleman and as a ruling elder for years in the Presbyterian Church, has done much to exalt this valley.

He has been superintendent of the Presbyterian Sunday School for the past twenty-one years—thus for more than a score of years he has been the principal in that religious school from which so many have passed into the church; into honorable vocations of life; into the better land.

About thirty-five years ago, Mr. Thompson married Miss Eva Keys. She was a daughter of the late John F. Keys, one of the early settlers of Cincinnati, against whose character not one word of reproach was ever uttered. He built the first brick house ever constructed in the city, and lived as a neighbor to the Lytles, the Burnets, and Longworths.

Her mother, Mrs. John F. Keys, is mentioned by Mrs. Charlotte Chambers Ludlow, wife of Colonel Israel Ludlow, in her memoirs, as having visited her at the old Ludlow Mansion, and enters her name on a list of friends, embracing such celebrated ladies as Mrs. General Lytle, Mrs. St. Clair, Mrs. Doctor Goforth, and others.

These pioneers of Glendale now reside in an elegant home on Magnolia Avenue. They have as companions in their advancing years, besides their dutiful children, nearly two thousand books in a well-selected library.

A THEOLOGICAL LIBRARY.

H. W. Hughes, Esq., is in possession of the

largest collection of theological works, as a part of his otherwise extensive and valuable library, to be found, doubtless, in the Miami valley. It numbers over two thousand volumes. His grandfather, Richard Hughes, lived in the North of Ireland. The Wesleys used to preach from the "upping block" in front of his house. He came to this country two years before the Revolution broke out, served as a soldier all through that war, and then settled in Virginia. The subject of this sketch was born in Virginia in 1814, came to Cincinnati 1848, and has been in the banking business ever since. He is now President of the Union National Bank, and an elder in the Presbyterian Church.

Mrs. Hughes is a niece to the late W. H. McGuffey, LL. D., and cousin to Rev. Dr. Joseph G. Monfort.

Mr. George Crawford, one of the pioneers of Glendale, built the present residence of Mr. Hughes, from whom he bought.

It stands on Greenville Avenue, facing the east, the spacious and beautiful grounds extending westward to the avenue in the rear.

Many beautiful pictures and paintings decorate the walls within, among them none more beautiful than "The Image Sellers," and a "Scene on Lake George," painted by a

daughter who not long since passed on to "the
land of light and beauty." "The Wise Men
and the Infant Jesus" is a very old painting,
and one very highly prized.

Mr. Hughes has the Bible bound in fifty
different editions. Upon a richly-carved table,
in the center of his parlor, the Bible and Shakspeare are constantly associated.

A SCHOLAR.

A few years ago the Ohio State Board of
School Examiners granted Florian Giauque,
Esq., a certificate to the effect that he was
qualified to teach in twenty-seven specified
branches. This was the highest number ever
enumerated in any certificate issued by such
Board. And none has equalled it since.
His ancestors came from Switzerland—a Republic for six hundred years, among "whose
rugged, snow-capped mountains the infant
Reformation was nutured." His father died
when he was eight years old, and his mother
nine years after. Then he was alone in the
world—but he was a student. At eighteen he
entered the Union army and served until the
close of the war. He graduated from Kenyon
College with the honors of his class. He was
subsequently principal of the Glendale public

schools for six years, during which time they rose to a rank never before attained. The course of study embraced higher branches then than have been prescribed by the Board of Education since.

After his creditable career as a teacher, he entered upon the practice of the law—his chosen profession—for which he had prepared himself while teaching. He is an archæologist, and as such has lectured and collected a choice cabinet of curiosities, consisting of stone weapons, ornaments, etc., mostly from Mill Creek Valley, which were on exhibition at the Centennial, and took the first premium at one of the Cincinnati Expositions.

While engaged in active practice at the Cincinnati Bar, he has written and compiled seven law books, which secured for him this commendation from Robert Clarke & Co. :

" The author is an able, careful, and accurate law writer. His works are classed among the most popular of recent publications, and are able and thorough expositions of the laws upon which they treat."

This gentleman is a representative of Mill Creek Valley in a scholastic sense, while in him Glendale has a scholar, a lecturer, a lawyer, an author and a mayor.

MR. THOMAS SPOONER

Is a direct descendant of William Spooner, the founder of a wide-spread and reputable family, who lived about the year 1637.

Reed Spooner (the father of Thomas) was "a man of strong and positive will, self-possessed, and commanded the high respect of all who knew him; was read in history and poetry, and was ambitious for the education of his children." He served with great credit to himself in the war of 1812.

Thomas Spooner was born January 17, 1817, in Cincinnati. His early days were spent in the city, but the greater part of his life was passed on his farm near Reading in this valley.

He has held many offices of trust, political and otherwise, and thus has contributed a considerable share to molding public character and forwarding public interests. He has the distinction of having been commissioned by President Lincoln Collector of Internal Revenue of the First District of Ohio, from 1862 to 1866. He may not have felled the forests and broken the stubborn glebe as a frontiersman, but he has rather been one of the many distinguished men of Hamilton County who pioneered educational, literary, and com-

mercial enterprises, whose services, though
not so arduous, are yet none the less essential
to the final consummation of all things that
pertain to making man complete as a physical,
intellectual, and moral being.

Mr. Spooner is spending the closing days of
his honorable life in a pleasant home on Sharon
Avenue, formerly the residence of the late
Samuel Fosdick.

DR. A. SHEPHERD'S

Residence is located in the very heart of the
village, being near the intersection of Myrtle
and Fountain avenues. The house was built
by Oliver S. Lovell, Esq., and was for some time
his home; for a while it was occupied by the
late Judge Miner and family, and subsequently
was purchased by Dr. Shepherd, who converted it into his beautiful home by greatly
enlarging and otherwise improving it.

To this lot belongs the distinction of having
upon it the largest elm tree in the village. It
measures sixteen feet around the trunk, which
tapers as gracefully as an obelisk for fifty feet
before a limb or a branch leaves it. It is probably two centuries old. Lightning has struck
it twice, shattering one of its branches, but its
huge body remained unscathed.

The "sharp and sulphurous bolt" may split " the unwedgeable and gnarled oak," but not the trunk of this ancient, monumental elm.

The doctor has a fine library (about five hundred volumes), and is a representative man in his profession, and especially in the chosen branch of homœopathy. He is, in fact, distinctively the pioneer of that branch of medicine in this valley. The doctor secured two degrees from eastern medical colleges; began the practice in Springdale in 1849, where he distinguished himself in treating cases of Asiatic cholera, and when he first introduced his specialty—homœopathic treatment. He removed to Glendale in 1867, where he now resides actively engaged in his chosen profession, in partnership with one of his sons, Dr. W. F. Shepherd; another son, Dr. A. L., being also a young practitioner in the city. Mrs. Dr. Shepherd has the distinction of being a granddaughter of the founder of Springdale—Col. Wm. Chamberlain, one of the earliest pioneers of this valley.

THE STONE MANSION,

Standing on the site of the old Heffner Tavern, on Fountain Avenue, is the home of

Mrs. S. B. Allen, widow of the late Samuel B. Allen, who was a son of Mr. Marston Allen, one of the most successful merchants in the early days of Cincinnati.

It is an imposing structure, and was seemingly built with regard to this sentiment found in Ruskin:

"The greatest glory in a building is not in its stones nor in its gold. Its glory is in its age, in that deep sense of voicefulness, of stern watching, of mysterious sympathy which we feel in walls that have long been washed by the waves of passing humanity."

Generations may come and go, but these walls will stand seemingly forever, at least until many a house within visual range of it shall have passed away or given place to others that shall rise upon their ruins.

THE FIRST LOT

Sold in Glendale, when the village was laid out, was bought by Dr. Henry Clark, for which he paid a premium of $500. The doctor soon after built the house which stands upon the lot at present, and is the home of his son, Mr. Albert G. Clark.

FROM THE TOWER

Of the beautiful residence of Mr. John H. Porter, a wonderful view may be obtained. Six Indian mounds may be seen within a radius of one mile; the Hamilton and Cincinnati pike almost to Chester Park, and from thence Clifton Avenue, until it passes over the hill at the Bellevue House; the two railroads in the valley, and the Cincinnati Northern, at times, on its way to Lebanon—a far, wide, wonderful view of the whole valley and all the clustered villages in the plains beneath.

A RIDE IN THE STAGE COACH,

Fifty years ago, by Mr. Richard W. Keys, should not go unmentioned. He left his father's house at daylight in the old stage, and journeyed over the old Wayne road, and, passing through this locality, reached Hamilton at 10 o'clock at night, on his way to Oxford. He recollects stopping at the old Heffner house.

His father was John F. Keys, Esq., one of the early day gentlemen of Cincinnati, whose old residence still stands next to the Cincinnati University.

Mr. Keys recollects seeing and shooting

wild turkeys on the hills north of his father's
house. He made maple sugar from the trees
which stood round about the old homestead.

MR. BENJAMIN STERRETT,

Now eighty years of age, lives in the retirement which wealth may afford, in a pleasant
house which he built on Fountain Avenue, in
1853. He was one of the first settlers in Glendale, probably the third.

He has had an active business career in
Cincinnati, in New York, and in Manchester,
England; finally succeeding in amassing a fortune, which enables him now to live a peaceful
but not an altogether retired life, for his heart
and hand are yet engaged in enterprises which
have for their object the good of others.

THE HOME

Of JUSTICE AND MRS. STANLEY MATTHEWS
is an object of interest to every visitor to Glendale.

The spacious, imposing house stands in the
center of about three acres, with Fountain
Avenue to the west and north, a cultivated
lawn sloping eastward, with many old trees,
deciduous and evergreen, and summer-houses

on wandering paths, as a part of the pleasures of this home.

Is it true that personal characteristics are sometimes imparted to that which a man builds and in which he lives as a home?

The foundations of this house are deep, and broad, and high; and he laid them just as he laid the foundations of his deep, and broad, and high character. The superstructure looks to all points of the compass, with almost the self-same equipose and outlines, as if, when the time would come, as it has, he would know no north, or south, or east, or west, in discharge of the lofty trust to which he is now called.

Above it towers a flag-staff. His attested patriotism is thus indexed by that silent shaft pointing ever to the unfaltering stars,

—" Argent,
And on an azure field "—

The sight of which, during all " the pangs of transformation," suggested to the fathers of the Republic the faultless fashion of that flag.

The most striking characteristic (not to speak of many that may be seen in the selection of paintings and other interior decorations) is its library room, in which are gathered about 2,500 volumes. Each of these books has contributed something to his scholarly attainments.

Upon the sides of that ever-rising, granitic pyramid of legal lore—the central structure of his vast and varied learning—the vines and flowers of literature climb and bloom, whose seeds were sown by a Shakspeare, a Dante, or a Goethe, and almost every other meritorious disseminator of thought—of every age, in every tongue.

"*At haec studia adolescentiam alunt, senectutem oblectant, secundas res ornant, adversis perfugium ac solacium praebent; delectant domi, non impediunt foris, pernoctant nobiscum, peregrinantur, rusticantur*"—"These studies employ youth, delight old age, adorn prosperity, afford a refuge and a solace in adversity; please at home, do not impede in the forum, go with us through the night, travel with us in the country."* Such are the pleasures of literature, portrayed by Cicero in his oration for the poet Archias.

We can not dwell upon any of the details of the brilliant career which led from a humble home in Cincinnati, where he was born July 21, 1824, to the bench of the Supreme Court

---

* Mansfield's "Personal Memories."

of the United States. But we may briefly say that his father was a Virginian and his mother the daughter of Colonel William Brown, one of the pioneers of this county. He, therefore, belongs to this valley, while he belongs to the Nation. Of him it has been said :—" For logical power, profound and varied learning, rare abilities of argument and persuasion, and high personal character, his has for more than a generation been *clarum et venerabile nomen.*"

The accomplished lady, whom he married—Miss Mary Black—has ever " swayed level in her husband's heart," since he began life as a young attorney in Tennessee until the present time ; and is now the central figure in the society of Washington, and whose absence from Glendale, even statedly, makes a social void none can fill.

This beautiful home is now occupied by MR. and MRS. MORTIMER MATTHEWS.

CHAPTER XX.

THE GLENDALE FEMALE COLLEGE,

AS an institution of learning, is a very important index to the growth of the valley, in this respect.

The building was designed for a hotel when first erected, but it was to be a seat of learning, not a summer resort. So it changed hands, passing to the Rev. John Covert in September, 1854, and was named " The American Female College." Two years afterwards it passed to Rev. J. G. Monfort, D.D., Rev. S. S. Potter, and Rev. L. D. Potter, who assumed management May 15, 1856.

That year the name was changed to the " Glendale Female College." Dr. Monfort was president nine years, leaving the institution after a successful administration, during which time it had become settled upon a secure basis with an enviable reputation. Thereupon Dr. Potter succeeded to the presidency, which position he has filled with distinction ever since.

From an address delivered by Dr. Potter,
June 12, 1879, we gather some facts which are
of interest, illustrating the work this noble
institution is doing:

"Of its graduates seventy-four have prominent places in churches and society; seventy-
three have been teachers; thirteen have distinguished themselves as authors and writers;
seven have married professors in our higher
institutions; and forty-six have married gentlemen in one of the learned professions. Several of those husbands (no doubt owing largely
to the influence of their wives, as is usually the
case) have risen to eminence in the army, in
their professions, and in other positions; one a
justice of the United States Supreme Court,
one a United States Minister to a foreign first-
class mission, and others in places of influence
in the churches; two have been members of
Congress, and two are foreign missionaries."

This college is on a firm footing, doing a
great and thorough work, having students from
all the neighboring States.

Dr. Potter was born in New Jersey in 1823.

The blood of the Ludlows is in his veins.
He graduated at Princeton College in 1841,
and finally completed a theological course at
the same college in 1846. For five years he

was in charge of the Presbyterian church in Brookville, Indiana. He was three years principal of the Whitewater Presbyterian Academy. Then moved to Glendale and became, as stated, connected with the management of this college, and subsequently its president.

Thus has he risen to this position. By hard study and continual experience as a teacher he became in every respect qualified for the trust. In 1844 the degree of M. A. was conferred upon him by old Princeton, and in 1872, that of D. D. by Hanover College, Indiana.

RELICS OF THE REVOLUTION.

During the war for our national independence, General Washington presented to Gen. Joseph Cilley, of New Hampshire, then serving upon his staff, a sword and a large, elegant silk sash, as a mark of personal esteem. At his death they passed to his son Jonathan, who emigrated to Ohio in 1803, and located a section of land in Colerain Township, where he died in 1807. The sash thereupon passed to his son Judge Jonathan Cilley, in whose possession it remained until his death, December 29, 1874, in Glendale.

His widow, Mrs. Judge Cilley, living upon

Sharon Avenue, is now the custodian of these interesting relics.

A LITERARY SOCIETY.

This village, on account of its many and extensive libraries, its college, public schools, and general literary accomplishments, will bear a comparison with "Melrose Abbey as a seat of learning" as well as with reference to its natural surrounding scenery.

This society has been in successful operation so long that it has become an institution of the village, and a brief notice, therefore, is necessary. For the past seven years, Mr. Geo. W. Gallager has been its active and efficient president, and in the discharge of his duties has evinced the executive ability of a Nichols and the aptitude of a Mapleson.

Of this society its president was once heard to utter, substantially, the following classic words in speaking of its members:

Polonius, "The best actors in the world, either for tragedy, comedy, history, pastoral, pastoral—comical, historical—pastoral, [tragical—historical, tragical—comical—historical— pastoral,] scene individible, or poem unlimited: Seneca cannot be too heavy, nor Plautus too light."

ST. GABRIEL'S CHURCH.

Was organized in 1858, and immediately afterwards a tasteful brick building was erected upon ground donated for that purpose by Messrs. Gross and Dietrich, at a cost of about three thousand dollars. The Rev. Father O'-Donnell has pastoral care of the same. Over two hundred pupils attend its parochial schools, kept by the Sisters of Charity in a building near the church.

CHRIST EPISCOPAL CHURCH.

This church movement was initiated August 6, 1865, by Rev. J. B. Pratt.

The families that aided him in his efforts were represented by Mr. and Mrs. Samuel Fosdick, Mr. and Mrs. John D. Jones, Col. and Mrs. Crafts J. Wright, Judge and Mrs. John L. Miner, Mr. and Mrs. R. M. Shoemaker, Mr. and Mrs. Wm. A. Proctor.

They at first worshipped in private houses; then in the school house; then built a little chapel on Sharon Avenue, upon the east side of Mr. Fosdick's lot.

Four years after its beginning it had built and paid for this costly edifice, and on the 30th day of May, 1869, the same was consecrated. By the side of this beautiful stone structure stands a rectory, also a tasteful building, the whole representing an expenditure of about $25,000. The Rev. Dr. Pise is now the minister in charge.

THE CHURCH OF THE NEW JERUSALEM (SWEDEN-BORGIAN).

Was built in 1860, costing about $7.000 The enterprise was first suggested by Mr. Charles H. Allen, who donated the ground upon which it stands.

Mr. Marston Allen contributed more liberally than any other person towards its construction.

It is a gothic structure, situated on Congress Avenue in the midst of old trees, whose overhanging branches shadow to solemnity this forest sanctuary set up within this grove which was God's temple long

> " Ere man learned to hew the shaft,
>   Or lay the architrave."

The Rev. Frank Sewell, of Urbana, preaches here regularly once a month.

THE PRESBYTERIAN CHURCH

Had its beginning in this immediate locality about seventy-five years ago, under the ministrations of the Rev. Robert Warwick, as elsewhere stated.

The following account of its formal organization in this village is from the pen of a gentleman who has been officially connected with it since that time:

At a meeting of a majority of the members of the First Presbyterian Church of Glendale, convened after due notice at the College chapel on Saturday evening, June 4, 1859, for the purpose of electing trustees and a clerk, and to become a body corporate under the laws of Ohio in such case provided, Samuel J. Thompson, Esq., was chosen chairman, and W. B. Probasco, Esq., was elected secretary.

On motion of Judge Matthews it was resolved that for the purpose of becoming a body corporate, the meeting proceed to elect three trustees and a clerk, to serve for the term of one year and until their successors shall be elected. Whereupon, the following gentlemen were nominated for trustees, and elected, viz: Richard W. Keys, Stanley Matthews, and W. B. Probasco; Samuel J. Thompson was nominated and elected clerk.

It was further resolved that the corporate name of said church be, "The First Presbyterian Church of Glendale."

W. B. PROBASCO.   S. J. THOMPSON,
     Secretary.   *Chairman.*

Received and recorded June 8, 1859, in Church Records Vol. I page 223, Hamilton County, Ohio.

Soon after this three elders were chosen, viz : John F. Keys, Wm. B. Moores, and J. J. Packer. Mr. Keys had been an elder for many years in the First Presbyterian Church of Cincinnati, and afterwards in the Seventh Presbyterian Church of Cincinnati. For several years the church occupied the chapel connected with the "Glendale Female College." For the first two years after its organization the church had no pastor; but there was preaching regularly by Rev. J. G. Monfort, D.D. and Rev. S. S. Potter.

Previous to the organization of the church, Rev. Thomas Spencer, a professor in the Female College, a man of eminent piety and scholarship, held religious services for a year or two in the chapel referred to, usually preaching himself; and at the same time established a Sunday School in the public school house. This was the beginning of the "Union Sabbath school " connected with the church. The first church edifice was built in 1859; and Rev. H. A. Tracy was unanimously elected pastor of the church in August 1861. He resigned in April, 1867, and was succeeded by Rev. W. H. Babbitt, who served the church faithfully for fourteen years, resigning his pastorate in October, 1881. The eldership from the beginning has embraced the following names: John F. Keys, J. J. Packer, W. B. Moores, W. B. Probasco, Stanley Matthews, Dr. Samuel Robbins, H. W. Hughes, Thomas J. Duncan, Thomas J. Biggs, Samuel J. Thompson. Elders Keys, Probasco, Moores, and Robbins have been removed by death. Judge Matthews retired upon his appointment to a seat on the Bench of the Supreme Court of the United States, and his consequent removal to Washington City. The others still remain in office.

In 1873 a new church edifice was erected at a cost of nearly $30,000, with a seating capacity of about 450; and the first building is now used as a chapel for prayer-meeting services and for the Sabbath school. The church membership numbers about 200, and the Sabbath school about 150, with an average attendance of 115 to 120. Mr. S. J. Thompson was elected superintendent of the school in January,

1862, and has been continuously in office, by annual re-election ever since.

For many years Judge Matthews was assistant superintendent, and a teacher in the school, but resigned these positions upon his election, as U. S. Senator.

A VIEW OF GLENDALE.

The writer was kindly permitted to see Glendale from the tower of COL. AND MRS. R. G. HUESTON'S stately residence.

The elevated ground upon which it stands, including adjoining farms to the east as far as the east branch of Mill creek, and to the south including Woodlawn and Beaumont Place, was, doubtless, an island in past ages when the great Miami was flowing through this valley.

Far as the eye can see to the north and east the ground rolls away, resembling a motionless, measureless, blue sea, over whose bosom

"The sunshine, masterless as wind,"

floats and sways like a golden veil, trailed by hands concealed in the empyrean.

Remnants of old forests may be seen ; cleared, cultivated fields ; comfortable homesteads,

near and remote; immense barns, where no
more may be heard

"The dull thunder of alternate flails."

But look westwardly to Glendale! Though
swept by hurricanes and devastated by fire,
still like a miniature Chicago rising resplen-
dently out of its own ashes—as if thriving
upon disaster. A beautiful vale has been cut
out by vast physical forces between this summit and that, sweeping eastwardly from the
southern limits of Glendale until it joins and
becomes a part of the valley formed by the
east fork of Mill creek. The railroad may be
seen winding its way from Woodlawn north-
wardly along the base of the ridge until it is
lost to view in the woodlands upon the Cochran farm. At stated times you can see the assembled equipages at the depot waiting for the
homeward bound residents, from whose feet
the dust of the city is nightly shaken. Then see
them evanish in the winding avenues!

See that solemn church pile in the fore-
ground, in whose every stone there is a sermon. Beyond that another—

"The gray spire molten now in driving mist,
Now lulled with the incommunicable blue."

There is the college whence a steady, pure, and noiseless stream of learning flows for the mental irrigation of the world. There are the clustered homes, half concealed and half disclosed, amidst embowering trees and luxuriant shrubbery.

"Far through the memory shines a happy day,
Cloudless of care, down-shod to every sense,
And simply perfect from its own resource."

That was when the writer saw Glendale for the first time, some twenty years ago.

AN ANTIQUARIAN.

There is a gentleman in Glendale who was born in Philadelphia in 1817. His mother was Mrs. Sarah A. Durang, daughter of Dr. J. Durang. He was a surgeon in the French army during the Revolution of 1766, under Louis XV. Dr. Durang came to this country in 1767, and located in Philadelphia. When Gen. LaFayette came to this country, he brought with other French regiments, the "Denalder," of which Dr. Durang was surgeon in France. The doctor thereupon joined his old regiment and served the young republic honorably and faithfully during the

Revolution. After independence was achieved, and during the great procession through Philadelphia, John Durang (son of the doctor) was dressed as Mercury, and stood on one of the printing presses and scattered odes to liberty. His dress, cap, and wings were prepared by Mrs. Beach, a daughter of Dr. Benjamin Franklin, the old philosopher himself being in the room while he was being thus attired.

Ferdinand Durang, another son, was at Fort McHenry during the bombardment by the English, Sept. 13, 1814.

It was upon this occasion that Francis Scott Key, while a prisoner upon an English man-of-war, was inspired to write "The Star Spangled Banner," by the sight of it as it floated above the fort. The words of the poem thrilled the soldiers, and all Baltimore. But what should be the music to those inspiring words? The problem was solved by Mr. F. Durang, and the story is thus told in an address delivered by Mr. Nathan Appleton on "The Star Spangled Banner," June 14, 1877, in Boston, Mass:

"'Have you heard Francis Key's poem?'" said one of our men as we lay scattered over the green hill near the captain's marquee. It was a rude copy, and written in a scrawl, which Horace Greeley might have mistaken for his own. He read it aloud, once, twice, three times, until the entire division seemed electrified by its pathetic eloquence. An idea seized Ferdinand Durang. Hunting up a volume of old flute music which was in somebody's tent, he impatiently whistled snatches of tune after tune, just as they caught his quick eye. One called 'Anacreon in Heaven' struck his fancy, and invited his attention Note after note fell from his puckered lips, until, with a leap and a shout, he exclaimed, ' Boys, I've hit it,' and fitting the tune to the words, there rang out for the first time the song of ' The Star Spangled Banner.' How the men shouted and clapped, for never was there a wedding of poetry to music made under such inspiring influences. Getting a brief furlough, the brothers sang it on the stage of Holliday Street Theatre soon after. It was caught up in the camps, and sung around our bivouac fires, and whistled in the streets, and when peace was declared, and we scattered to our homes, carried to thousands of firesides, as the most precious relic of the war of 1812."

The veritable flag that floated over Fort McHenry was on exhibition at the time of Mr. Appleton's address, and this antiquarian has a photograph of it. His father's father was a soldier in the Revolution, and was killed at the battle of Germantown. His father was a " cunning artificer " of Philadelphia, an insight into whose skill and ingenuity may be obtained by looking upon the relics now constituting a part of the "Cabinet of Curiosities" found in the cozy cottage home of Mr. Geo. W. GALLAGER on Greenville Avenue.

When the Glaciers ploughed out this valley they left three large old red sandstone bowlders on this lot. This was in accordance with the eternal fitness of things, for sometime afterwards it became the home of this antiquarian. These strange stones became the nucleus of a collection of geological curiosities, to which specimens have been constantly added since 1864, at which time this antiquarian acquired title to this lot and its bowlders.

And to this cabinet have been added numberless relics from every other imaginable field :

A lock of hair from the head of *Na-pa-shin*, one of the thirty-eight Indians hung in Minnesota Dec. 26, 1862, and who boasted he had killed twenty-six white men.

A cannon ball fired into the " Anglo-Saxon" when she passed Vicksburg during the Rebellion.

Piece of the Cathedral bell at Monterey, Mexico, shattered by a ball from Gen. Worth's division.

Three earthen faces, (burnt clay) taken from Pyramid of Cholula, Mexico, constructed by the Toltecs, about the seventh century.

A howitzer, about twenty-five pounds in weight, made of rebel bullets fired into Fort Sedgwick Dec. 29, 1864, Petersburg, Va.

Gun Lock, ninety-five years under water in the Delaware River, on the "Augusta," sunk while trying to convey supplies to the English army.

Holbein's Dance of Death, carved in Switzerland, 1496.

Piece of Charter Oak, which stood, 1689, in Hartford, Connecticut.

Piece of Penn Treaty elm.

History of Franklin Pierce, one inch and a half long, and one wide, 14 pp., about 120 mo.

Piece of flag-staff, captured by General Scott at Vera Cruz.

Washington Penny, 1791, very rare.

Pine Tree Shilling, 1672, first coin struck off in this country.

Coin issued by the Moors when they entered Spain in the seventh century.

Commission as Brigadier-General, issued by General JAMES H. BAKER, his brother-in-law, to GEORGE WASHINGTON GALLAGER for gallant services during the war *in Glendale*.

THE ALLENS

Have done much to improve Glendale. Mr. Marston Allen, the father, was an eastern gentleman, coming to Cincinnati in 1818. After a successful business career he retired to this place in 1853, built the residence now occupied by Mrs. George Shillito, invested his means in other ways, was one of the signers to the petition for incorporating the village, and lived in the quiet and ease which wealth affords until 1868, when he died at the age of eighty years.

CHARLES H. ALLEN, ESQ.,

Has invested largely in and around Glendale. About 100 acres of this beautiful country belongs to him. His homestead stands on a commanding point, looking south from Fountain Avenue. A porch along its entire front ornamented by columns, it is an imposing feature, while around its balustraded roof one can walk as upon a castle's walls.

This house may be distinctly seen from Clifton and other points even more remote to the south.

THE DISTINGUISHED NAMES

Met with in the early history of this immediate locality, touching the title, church chronicles, act of incorporation, etc., are—
Judge John C. Symmes. Col. John Riddle.
Hon. Alex. Hamilton. Major Joseph Harris.
Elder Robt. Burns. Rev. Robt. Warwick.
Mr. Samuel Adams. Elder John Hunter.

THE INCORPORATION

Of Glendale was finally effected March 13, 1855. R. C. Phillips, Esq., was the surveyor. While thus engaged, he had his office in a little frame house still standing on the east side of the pike, south of the toll gate. Thirty persons signed the petition asking to be incorporated. Of these only six are at present living there:
Justice S. Matthews. S. J. Thompson, Esq.
Mr. Benjamin Sterrett. Chas. H. Allen, Esq.
Mr. Reed Bartlett. John K. Sterrett, Esq.

HON. W. M. BATEMAN

Is a representative man, in a professional sense, of the Miami Valley. He studied law with Governor Corwin, and has been a steady and successful practitioner of the same to the present time. He was United States District Attorney during the whole of President Grant's administration, was State Senator from Hamilton County, and has always exercised great influence in public circles. His handsome residence is on the east side of Ivy Avenue, which he built in 1859. He has collected together about fifteen hundred books in his library, and he is thoroughly acquainted with their contents. While devoted to the law, he yet so loves the paths of literature, that he never hesitates to make a detour into those rich realms, always returning, however, the better equipped for the stern and solemn duties of an exacting and jealous profession.

MURRAY C. SHOEMAKER, ESQ.,

Is the son of Col. R. M. Shoemaker (at one time mayor of Glendale) and lives in his father's summer residence on the south side of Fountain Avenue.

R. M. Shoemaker, Esq., is one of the rail-road kings of the West. He engineered the laying out and the construction of the C. H. & D. R. R., the Dayton Short Line, and the Dayton and Michigan ; was President of the Cincinnati Southern for awhile, built four hundred miles of the Union Pacific ; and all his life has been an energetic, leading man in those tremendous agencies that have hastened the development of this valley and the country at large.

Mr. S. is spending the last years of his eventful life in the late home of Judge Este on West Fourth street, which property he bought out of his ample fortune.

It should be added that he was President of the C. H. & D. and the Dayton Short Line for a number of years.

WM. A. PROCTER, ESQ.,

Owns a farm adjoining Glendale immediately on the east. The stately homestead, with its white walls, broad porch, lofty columns, and wide-spreading lawn, cultivated far away to the front beneath the old forest trees whose kingly presence is felt as you stand beneath them, completely symbolizes the idea of a rural retreat from the factory-full city to the south.

COL. C. W. MOULTON,

The head of the Cincinnati law firm, Moulton, Johnson and Levy, is also a representative man of this valley.

His home is on Fountain Avenue next north of the Presbyterian Church, and abounds in pictures, statuary, books, and every thing that can lend a refining and an elevating influence to the fireside. There are about fifteen hundred books in his private library, not to speak of the law books. Next to the Lincoln library, his is the largest collection of law books at the Cincinnati Bar.

Mrs. Moulton belongs to one of the most distinguished families in the United States. She is a sister to General and Senator Sherman, and by marriage connected with the almost royal family of the late Thomas Ewing, whose fine portrait adorns Col. Moulton's library.

J. H. BARRETT, ESQ.,

Superintendent of the C. H. and D. Rail-

road, resides on Greenville Avenue. He is
a representative of this powerful organization
which supplies the arterial blood for the many
municipal corporations which have sprung up
along its course through the Miami valley, and
but for which they would never have had an
existence.

DR. R. B. MUSSEY

Is living in the Harkness property fronting
east on Laurel Avenue. This is a landmark of
the village. It was built by Mr. Anthony
Harkness about 1853, and possesses some of
his characteristics. Mrs. Mussey is a daughter
of Col. Charles L. Gano, and a grand-
daughter of Mr. Harkness. The pioneers of
the valley are thus well represented in the
residents of this family homestead.

HON. CHANNING RICHARDS.

This gentleman is at present United States
District Attorney for the Southern District of
Ohio, and as such is a representative man of
the Miami, and especially the Mill creek valley. He lives in a pleasant home on the north
side of Sharon Avenue.

THE HOMES OF GLENDALE.

MR. ALFRED G. ALLEN, one of the sons of the late Marston Allen, has a beautiful cottage villa in the margin of an old forest on Congress Avenue.

MR. N. GOLDSMITH has a delightful home on east Fountain Avenue, in a two-and-a-half acre lot, most beautifully located.

MR. SAMUEL McCUNE, late mayor of Glendale, resides in a tasteful home, with verandas, bay windows, and French roof, facing south on Wood Avenue. Immediately opposite is the home of Robert Clarke, Esq.

JOHN D. JONES, ESQ., resides on Wood and Congress avenues. It is a very noticeable brick structure, surrounded by luxuriant shrubbery. Many old trees are in the lot to the west of the home. The name of the late John D. Jones, his father, is most honorably associated with the early history of Cincinnati.

MR. CHARLES DAVIS has his summer residence here, and a remarkably beautiful one. It stands on a lot containing six acres, on the corner of Erie and Forest avenues. Choice fruits, flowers, plants, and shrubbery are cultivated here, without regard to the cost, and, as a pleasure resort, abounds with the most elevating and refining suggestions and influences.

The late JAMES F. CUNNINGHAM, a pioneer of this valley and of the Methodist Church, lived until a year ago in the beautiful residence now standing, and which he built, on the southeast corner of Arbor Place and Sharon Avenue.

THE HARKNESS HOMESTEAD, built by the late Anthony Harkness, Esq., stands as a landmark fronting east on Laurel Avenue.

WM. WILSON MCGREW ESQ., lives in a handsome frame on Forest Avenue.

MR. JAMES C. RICHARDSON occupies the Haldeman homestead, and MR. W. S. GRANDIN that built originally by R. B. Moores. These constitute a park in and of themselves, extending from Willow to Laurel, and from Fountain to Sharon avenues.

MRS. M. S. PATTERSON's residence is on Sharon Avenue, being the splendid home at one time of Daniel DeCamp, Esq.

DR. JOHN and JAMES PATTERSON are the sons of Mrs. Patterson, and have their office on these premises.

MRS. ROBERT CRAWFORD is the oldest resident of the village. Her maiden name was Anna Lemon. She was born Nov. 1, 1797, near North Bend. Her father was a carpenter, and built Judge Symmes' house at that place. She remembers seeing Judge Symmes, and can describe his appearance.

Mrs. Crawford is an interesting character in the history of Glendale. She lives in the enjoyment of remarkably good health at her advanced age in the home built by Mr. Crawford in 1853.

Mr. and Mrs. Clinton Kirby, descendants of the Kirby and Crawford families, distinguished in the history of the country for intelligence and wealth, are also occupants of the Crawford homestead, a beautiful place, with an orchard and meadow around it.

Mrs. Daniel McLaren's elegant residence stands on Greenville Avenue. It was originally built by Mr. Daniel DeCamp, and always attracts the attention of the visitor to Glendale. Mrs. McLaren has an extensive library, numbering about one thousand volumes. It is a beautiful house.

Mr. W. C. Howard, clerk of the United States District Court, has recently purchased a pleasant home on Magnolia Avenue.

DR. AND MRS. PATTERSON

Live in a comfortable home between Magnolia and Ivy avenues, not far from the residence of the Hon. W. M. Bateman.

THE PUBLIC SCHOOLS

Are of a high order. The buildings are located on Congress Avenue. Professor Giauque, was principal six years. He was succeeded by Prof. H. B. McClure, a fine scholar (now the law partner of Prof. Giauque) who was followed by Prof. R. H. Whallon, now in charge. Mr. Whallon is a well educated gentleman, and is maintaining the high standard set up by his predecessors. There are about two hundred pupils and five teachers in the school.

THE POST OFFICE is in charge of Miss Sallie E. Russell, who is now serving under the third administration since her appointment.

WALTER E. BONNELL is station agent, the depot being a solid brick building, which was recently constructed in place of the frame destroyed by fire a few years since.

THE STORES

Are kept by Mr. W. P. Bruce and Wm. Lehrer Co., on Fountain Avenue, and Mr. Maher on Sharon Avenue. Thus in the matter of markets, dry goods, groceries, daily mails, telegraphs, telephones, etc., this village has first-class advantages.

THE RESIDENTS

Of the valley, not elsewhere named, who have procured homes in this village, are:

Thos. J. Biggs, Esq.   Mr. John Titus.
Mr. Henry Cilley.   H. W. Hughes, Jr.
Mrs. W. B. Probasco.   Mr. Daniel McLaren.
Mrs. M. Kinmont.   J. B. Stoughton, Esq.
Mr. J. B. C. Moores.   Mrs. Fenton Lawson.
Reed Bartlett, Esq.   H. R. Probasco, Esq.
Michael Dooley, Esq.   Mr. Harry Willis.
S. T. Crawford, Esq.   Mr. N. L. Barnard.
Mr. E. L. Loweree.   Mrs. F. M. Douglass.
Mrs. B. R. Stevens.   Chas. E. Spinning, Esq.
Thos. J. Duncan, Esq. W. St. John Jones, Esq.
A. W. Ross, Esq.   C. W. McIntyre, Esq.
Mr. John K. Sterrett.   C. W. Withenbury, Esq.
Prof. E. Y. Robbins.   Mr. Thos. Johnson.

THE COCHRAN FARM.

To the north of Glendale is a splendid landed estate, belonging to the Hon. John M. Cochran, one of the most highly respected citizens of this valley. Mr. Cochran descends from Hon. Jeremiah Morrow, once Governor of Ohio. He has served the county three terms in the Ohio Legislature, has been entrusted with the settlement of large estates, and in these stations has never betrayed a trust. His splendid farm is in a high state of cultivation, and is the home of wealth and contentment.

THE BUGHER FARM.

An account of the early settlement of this farm may be seen on page 42-3.

In the old grave-yard, near the railroad, two fallen tombstones read thus:

In memory
of
HENRY TUCKER,
Who died Sept, 28, 1844, aged 84 yrs.
He was one of the first settlers in Ohio.

In memory
of
MARY TUCKER,
Died Dec. 16, 1848, age, 88 yrs.

This venerable couple were thus born in the same year, 1760. Having struggled to clear this rich and beautiful land, they now rest from their labor.

" The cock's shrill clarion, or the echoing horn
No more shall rouse them from their lowly bed."

This farm now belongs to Mr. Horace Bugher, who uses it mainly for the purpose of cultivating fine stock of all kinds. As such it is a conspicuous illustration of growth in this direction.

CHAPTER XXI.

SPRINGDALE.

WE can not devote the space to this interesting locality that it deserves.

About the year 1820 it was the most important and wealthy village in the county. It maintained that rank until 1851, when the construction of the C. H. & D. Railroad—so near and yet so far—took its prestige away, and indeed blighted its further growth.

In 1841 it had fifty-five dwellings, four stores, two taverns, one school-house, one church, and a large number of mechanic shops.

It has no more of either now. But it is interesting even in its old habilaments. The country around it is incomparably rich in soil and beautiful in contour. The farms are in a high state of cultivation.

Many noted names connected with the settlement of this valley are to be found in tracing the history of Springdale:

Hon. O. P. Morton was born here; Col.

Wm. Chamberlain ; Major John Baldwin ; John McGilliard, Justice of the Peace in 1807 ; Capt. John Brownson, U. S. A., John Rogers, Wm. Creager, G. W. Wilmuth, Hatfield Williams, Caleb Crane, and, still later, Dr. John R. Hunt, whose venerable and accomplished widow still lives in refined retirement in the village. We insert this just tribute to Dr. Hunt from the pen of his gifted son, the Honorable Samuel F. Hunt, himself being a distinguished representative of this valley, now of the Cincinnati Bar. It is an extract from an address delivered by Gen. Hunt at Hamilton, on " The Miami Valley," July 4, 1881.

" There are, too, recollections and sympathies of a more tender nature which impelled me to come. My father, more than fifty years ago, after leaving Nassau Hall and the College of Physicians and Surgeons in New York, came to the Miami Valley. For forty years he continued in the practice of his profession. He now sleeps in the village church-yard at Springdale, on the very ground where stood the pioneer church of 1796, and left behind him a memory which is cherished in the whole community as that of a good physician, a kind father, and an estimable friend and fellow-citizen."

THE PRESBYTERIAN CHURCH

Is the growth from seed sown April 4, 1796. Subscriptions for "a Grave-yard and Meeting-house" were started at that date, the following being evidence of the fact:—

We, whose names are hereto affixed, do promise to pay or cause to be paid unto Mr. John Schooley, Mr. William Preston, or Luke Foster, the several sums annexed to our names, in cash or labor, for the use of procuring a piece of land for a grave-yard, and to defray the expense of a temporary meeting-house for the Presbyterian society of this Township of Springfield, on demand, this fourth day of April, 1796 :

NAMES.	DAYS.	LABOR.	CASH.
John Schooley............	2	Team.	£1 10s od
Levy Sayre................	2		15 0

This church was a "large frame building, nearly square, with galleries on the three sides, and the pulpit at the north end." It was com-in 1801-2.

The present brick building was erected in 1834. This church has done great good in the valley. Its old records are bright with names long since "written in heaven." We can not pause to name all who have labored in ministry and laity within its walls. He who is the Invisible sees and knows all. The Rev. Wm. H. James is now in charge of this historic church. He assumed charge July 29, 1866, and is a graduate of Princeton Theological

Seminary. We take great pleasure in giving
room to this just tribute to Mr. James, from
the pen of Mr. Olden :—

" Without ostentation, but with unremitting labor, Mr.
James has served the church for more than sixteen years, and,
if a steady increase of membership and uninterrupted harmony in the church and among the congregation are to be
taken as evidence, his ministerial labors have been crowned
with more than ordinary success. He has surely secured to
himself the confidence and esteem, not only of his congregation, but the entire community in which he resides."

MRS. DR. JOHN R. HUNT

Resides in a comfortable home on the main
thoroughfare of the village. This has been
the scene of hospitality and refinement for more
than fifty years. How could it well be otherwise, connected as she is with the Pendletons,
and back of them, with Revolutionary ancestors who fought on the fields of Princeton and
Monmouth for the peace and independence
which the Republic enjoys to-day.

HON. CHESTER M. POOR,

At present a Representative from this county
to the Legislature, cultivates a finely stocked
farm just north of the village. Upon it the
Hon. O. P. Morton was born ; over it passed
Wayne's army ; and near its north line Col.
Elliott was massacred.

CHAPTER XXII.

LOCKLAND

I s a manufacturing village. No place of its population exceeds it as such. Two railroads pass through it, the Miami canal, and many other thoroughfares in all directions. An immense amount of capital is invested here in its manufactories and mills. It began its career in 1829, when Nicholas Longworth and Louis Howell laid out the town. It is younger than the Miami canal, for when it was constructed there were only two houses there. In 1880 it had eighteen hundred and eighty-six inhabitants. It is partly in Springfield and partly in Sycamore townships. It was incorporated December 20, 1865.

Here are the celebrated Paper Mills of Friend and Fox; the two mills of Haldeman Paper Co.; the Tangeman Paper Mills; Geo. H. Friend's Paper Mills; the Geo. Fox Starch Factory; the Flour Mills of Palmer Bros. & House; the Lockland Lumber Co., belonging

to Geo. S. Stearns & Sons, and the Cotton
Factory, operated by Stearns and Foster.

The Wayne Avenue church, described on
page 118, is in this village. It had its beginning
in 1799, when a Methodist class-meeting was
held for the first time at the house of Mr. Ram-
sey by Rev. Francis McCormick. The Presbyterian church, as a branch of the Reading
church, began April 6, 1850. The Rev. Benjamin Graves was its first preacher. The Rev.
S. C. Palmer is in charge at present. Rev.
J. W. Davis is pastor of the Baptist church.

There are many wealthy business men in
this little city :

Mr. John H. Tangeman has a large paper
mill, giving employment to many persons, a
brief sketch of whom appears in the chapter
on Wyoming.

Mr. James C. Richardson, president of the
Haldeman Paper Co., residing in Glendale.

Mr. Gideon G. Palmer, also referred to in
the article on Wyoming, Mr. C. D. Palmer,
and Mr. George House, constituting the firm
or G. G. Palmer and Co.

Mr. George H. Friend, Mr. Thomas Fox,
and many others.

The legal profession is represented by
William Cornell, Esq.

The medical profession by Dr. Highland, Dr. J. T. Booth, and Dr. John Anderson.

The new public school building, approaching completion, will be one of the finest and largest in the valley. Prof. J. M. Miller has been principal of this school over thirteen years.

There are some beautiful homes here. That of MR. and MRS. THOMAS FOX is a representative. They were born, respectively, in 1822, and 1823, were baptized by the same minister, and ultimately married by him—the Rev. W. H. Raper—and are both natives of the Miami Valley. Mrs. Fox planned their present elegant home. It was built in 1860—a tasteful brick structure, painted dark green with red trimmings. It is the home of many pictures and books.

MR. GEORGE H. FRIEND has a pleasant home on Wayne Avenue, built in 1853. The grounds embrace about four acres. He is the proprietor of three large paper mills.

He has endured many hardships and losses in his business career, but has persevered until he is one of the foremost manufacturers of paper in the valley. His strong convictions and adherence to political principles brought him into local prominence as an opponent or slavery years before the war.

JOHN GANO OLDEN, ESQ., for a long time a resident of Lockland, was born near Glendale on the old Morse farm, in 1819. His mother was a daughter of Wm. Gano, whose father was a brother of General John Gano, the founder of a distinguished family in Hamilton county. It will be remembered that the blood of the Huguenots courses the veins of this family.

Mr. Olden is a pioneer who has won distinction heretofore in another than the actual field of a frontiersman's life. His literary tastes and achievements have done much to render his name a household word in Mill Creek Valley.

He has a pleasant country home on old Wayne Avenue, but is at present residing in Cincinnati.

The following are the names of some of the prominent citizens who have built residences in this villiage:

Charles S. Dunn, Esq., who has served as mayor, altogether, about eleven years.

Joseph Sampson.   Jos. W. Thomas, Esq.
Mrs. Rebecca Bachelor. W. S. Bacon, Esq.
Mr. R. B. Latta.   Mr. Henry Gilbert.
Capt. G. W. Walker. Mr. Issac Skillman.
J. F. Pendery, Esq.   Philip Grosh, Esq.
Mr. D. D. Thompson. John G. Lyons.

Albert Lyons.   Adam Schwartz.
John J. Smiley, Esq.   Leander Warren, Esq.
Herbert Sullivan, Esq. Dan Mitchell, Esq.
Jacob French, Esq.   Mr. John Buchanan.
Mr. Theo. Skillman.   W. A. Thomas, Esq.
Adolphus Smith, Esq.   Lewis Dehmel, Esq.

The Lockland and Wyoming Improvement Co., of which the Hon. Robert Hosea is President, has also built several beautiful houses on its fine property, situated on both sides of the C. H. & D. Railroad.

J. C. Bellew, Esq., is at present Mayor of Lockland.

CHAPTER XXIII.

WINTON PLACE

IS a sprightly suburb immediately north of Spring Grove cemetery. Many costly and delightful homes are to be found here. It has had a wonderful growth, and recently became an incorporated village. It was planned in 1865 by Messrs. Hand and Froome. The celebrated Platt Evans owned the fine ground east of the railroad.

The following gentlemen have located their home here and in this vicinity.

HON. JACOB BURNET, late judge of the Common Pleas Court.

JUDGE F. W. MOORE, now on the Common Pleas Bench.

SAMUEL HANNAFORD, ESQ., widely known as an architect, and at present superintendent of the new Custom House.

PROF. SAMUEL W. WILLIAMS, one of the finest classical scholars and best read gentlemen in the West. He has a library of choice old and new books, numbering about twenty-five hundred volumes.

HON. W. M. YEATMAN, at present State Senator for Hamilton county.

MR. D. W. MILLER, member of the Cinnati Bar.

ARTHUR G. MOORE, ESQ., superintendent of the Cincinnati water works.

GEN. CHAS. E. BROWN, member of the Bar, and a distinguished soldier, who lost a leg at Atlanta, July 22, 1864.

Hon. D. W. Miller.	Edwin Anderson, Esq.,
Dr. W. P. Runkle,	G. W. Sholl, Esq.
Dr. P. F. Maley.	R. P. Harkness, Esq.
H. H. Vail, Esq.,	Mr. Lovett,
Frank A. Armstrong.	Mrs. Sarah Meyer.
Robert Smith, Esq.	G. W. Harris, Esq.
Mr. Wm. Innis.	Mrs. Thomas Holliday.

Mrs. Samuel Froome.

CHAPTER XXIV.

CARTHAGE.

As to this important village, it may be said that there is an ancient and modern Carthage. Part of it is very old, part of it is new.

Many historical associations cluster about its earlier days. Many references have been made to them in these pages. The settlement of this valley began at White's Station, now in the corporate limits.

It was laid out as a town in 1815, by Edward White, sometimes called Edward III. It was quite an important village before the canal and railroad came.

The situation is extremely advantageous for access to the city. Its soil is rich and dry. The surrounding country beautiful. Its healthfulness beyond question. There are already many pleasant attractive homes there.

THE McCAMMONS have pleasant homes, in the midst of flowers, plants and shrubbery, on Second Avenue.

Capt. F. A. Myer's cottage, on Main avenue, is strikingly beautiful and unique in design.

Capt. C. A. Santmyer, first earned the peace a home affords, on the battle-fields of his country; then married Miss Helen M. Wright, a descendant of the venerable pioneer, Dr. Thos. Wright; and then found that home in this village.

Jonathan R. Bonnell, one of the oldest residents, lives in quietude and among friends on the corner of Jackson and Second streets.

Mr. William Brickley is superintendent of the public schools.

Mr. Joseph W. Henry, postmaster, lives comfortably on Main Avenue.

Mr. John Critchell is a member of the Board of Education.

Mrs. Jacob Billingsly. Hon. John G. Sextro.
J. W. Sprung, Esq. B. P. Critchell, Esq.
R. C. Phillips (at one time mayor of Carthage)
Mr. Henry Varwig. Mrs. Charles Howell.
Mr. John Belser. Mrs. I. W. Bacon.
Thomas Southwell. Mr. John Gibson.
Col. Thomas Hunt. Maj. J. Stewart, U.S.A.

The following gentlemen represent the medical profession:
Dr. A. Smedley. Dr. A. B. Luse.
Dr. T. S. Potter. Dr. Willis Saffin.

The legal profession is represented by—
Capt. Smith Stimmel. W. Hartley Pugh, Esq.

G. A. R.

Many old soldiers meet here, under this
name. It is the R. L. McCook post, of which
Capt. Santmyer is commander. It is in possession of a valuable portrait of General Mc-
Cook, presented by the members of that celebrated family.

RAILROADS AND OTHER ROADS.

The site of Carthage was first known as
"The Third Crossing of Mill Creek," or
White's Station. That was reached from Cincinnati by the old Wayne road, in 1791-2.
The next road laid out was the new Hamilton
road, in 1817, which pursued the track of the
Wayne trace to where Gas Hall now stands,
then diverged to the north and west, and pursued a direct course along section lines until
it intersected the Wayne road again at a point
in Glendale, near the toll-gate.

The Miami canal came next in point of time
—1827 ; then the C. H. and D., Railroad, in
1852 ; then the Dayton Short Line, in 1870.

When the cars commenced running on the C. H. and D., there were but three passenger and three freight trains each way. Now sixty freight and passenger trains run daily over this road; and sixteen passenger trains over the Short Line.

No suburb of Cincinnati surpasses this in railroad facilities.

THE CARTHAGE MILLS,

Of which Mr. Howard B. Hills is the proprietor, deserves mention as being the outgrowth of the old grist-mill formerly built and managed by Major Caldwell about the year 1806. It stood within sight of this location, and but a short distance to the north-west. This old mill was swept away by a flood, which forced its way from the main bed of the creek through the mill race; and such was its suddenness that Major Caldwell had barely time to escape being carried away with the mill. He made his escape from the moving wreck by a bold and successful leap for the bank.

This is a complete little mill, built of brick, and operated by steam, and yielding about forty-five barrels of flour per day.

About thirty thousand dollars are invested in this enterprise.

DISTILLERIES.

Old Capt. Jacob White raised the second crop of corn cultivated by the pioneers in this valley. And it is elsewhere stated that probably the first distillery erected on Mill Creek was that upon the Caldwell farm, west of Carthage, over eighty years ago. As a grain-growing region, it has a striking illustration in the magnitude of the distilling interests which have grown up since that time.

The Mill Creek Distilling Co. (formerly J. W. Gaff & Co.) occupies sixteen acres at the mouth of Mill Creek. The distillery has a working capacity of 16,000 gallons per day, which, at ninety cents per gallon, would yield a daily tax of $14,400, or over $4,000,000 annually—more than one-fortieth of the entire revenue collected by the United States.

H. B. HILLS, ESQ.,

Is the son of the venerable pioneer Townsend Hills, Esq. He is developing this valley by way of building a tasteful home.

His lot fronts 226 feet on the north side of Second street.

There are full-grown shade trees about this

building site—a part of the grove elsewhere spoken of, which has a deeply interesting history.

That the future of Carthage is promising may be gathered from the fact that such gentlemen as Mr. Hills, Col. Ward, Major Gibson, the McCammons, and others, have expended so largely of their means in building their homes here.

Thus MR. AND MRS. HILLS, by an expenditure of about seven thousand dollars, have provided themselves a lovely retreat,

"In the deep umbrage of the beech tree's shade,
Which shows a distant prospect far away of busy cities."

GAS HALL.

The rapid growth of this country can not be better illustrated than by allusion to this building, erected by the Cincinnati Gas Light and Coke Company at a cost of $75,000.

COL. GEORGE WARD,

During the year 1881, completed one of the finest residences in this valley. It faces north on what is now known as Fifth Avenue in Carthage, being immediately west of the C. H. & D. Railroad.

This avenue was formerly known as the North Bend road; but before that it was an old Indian trail from one Miami River to the other. Griffin's Station was but a few hundred feet north of it.

In looking at this elegant home, that of another came to mind, now known only to the historian. The wide hall, lofty ceilings, spacious and communicating rooms, furnished withal in a manner so munificent, with the sound of falling waters like unwritten music breaking in upon the stillness of the night—no effort of the imagination was required, nor was it a violent exercise of it, to institute a comparison between it and the "Island mansion" of the refined, but ill-fated Blannerhassetts.

Sitting upon that veranda one moonlight evening, and contemplating the beautiful landscape to the north and west, embracing the ridge of hills that stretches away to Glendale, these words floated through the memory:

—"To me
High mountains are a feeling, but the hum
Of human cities torture! I can see
Nothing to loathe in nature, save to be
A link reluctant in a fleshly chain."

THE GIBSON RESIDENCE

Is one of the most conspicuous houses on

Second Avenue, rendered such by its bold tower, surmounted by a shaft from whose top, now and then, floats the flag ·· whose hues were born in heaven.''

This is a very large and superior house, and is the pleasant, refined home of MAJOR and MRS. H. B. GIBSON.

Upon entering these grounds BARRY CORN-WALL would have said :

" I come
To this sweet place for quiet ;
Every tree, and bush, and fragrant flower,
That flings unto the winds its morning incense
Is my friend.''

JOHN M'CAMMON

Was born March 9, 1814, at Shippensburg, Pa. He came to Cincinnati with his father in 1816. March, 1821, his father's family came to Carthage. He united with the Christian Church in 1833, under the ministrations of the Rev. Walter Scott, and thereupon and thenceforth became an active worker in all Christian enterprises. June 14, 1840, he married Miss Joanna Bonnell.

They lived together forty-two years, when he died at Carthage April 1, 1882.

Thus another pioneer has passed away!
Let us note his fall.

He was a Christian. The history of his church attests that. He was a patriot—none truer than he during the dark hours of the war. He was an honest man. Hear the Hon. Julius Dexter at the dedication of Music Hall May 15, 1878:

"I must mention the honest, faithful, careful superintendent, whom neither fear nor favor can cause to swerve. He has watched this building from its lowest foundation stone to its highest pinnacle with an eye single to his duty, that the hall should be what it is—safe. For that sense of security which you have a right to feel within these walls, thank JOHN McCAMMON."

It may be said of him, as it was said of the elder Chatham—"Modern degeneracy had not reached him."

Content with honest toil and its reward; gentle and contemplative in disposition; fond of the fellowship of the good; a lover of the beautiful in art, and song, and poetry; a fond father in a happy home; a PIONEER in many a sense of the term, he lived an honorable and useful life and died the death of the righteous.

Many a musing mourner followed him to his grave, and many a year will elapse before his

honored name will fade from the memory of
men.

CAPT. JACOB WHITE.

This sturdy, resolute, and remarkable man
—this foremost pioneer in the settlement of this
valley north of the Ludlow settlement—was
born May 2, 1759, in New Jersey. His wife,
Joanna Mounts, who came with him and
shared his toils and dangers, was born Nov. 6,
1760. They were married Oct. 25, 1780.
Nine years afterwards they came to Cincinnati,
and, July 23, 1792, located Sect. 1, Springfield
Township.

This section includes the northern part of
Carthage and the present site of Hartwell and
Maplewood. He built the block-house, elsewhere mentioned, on the banks of Mill creek.
He subsequently built a hewed log-house
(1798) near the present residence of Major
Stewart, the railroad destroying its exact site.
By hard and hazardous toil, he succeeded in
clearing and improving this section; his saw
and grist-mill being a famous resort in its time.
But misfortune overtook him. The United
States Bank looked to his valuable estate to
make good his endorsement for a neighbor and
friend, and shortly afterward it was swept
away from him.

Capt White moved to Gallatin County, Kentucky, about the year 1838. He died July 20, 1849, ninety-three years of age.

MRS. NANCY WHITE CULBERTSON,

His grand-daughter, the last of this family in this vicinity, now resides in Carthage. She is the daughter of Providence White, and was born May. 20, 1810. Her father lived on the Cilley farm from 1810 to 1832, and built the house that formerly stood in front of the present residence of Major Cormany. He first lived in a double log cabin that stood a short distance west, the foundations of which were torn away when Ridgeway Avenue was constructed. Around that old cabin stood an apple orchard, which Mrs. Culbertson says, was the first orchard planted between the Miami rivers.

She is alone—but not comfortless—with her old family-Bible and its record of births and deaths, admonishing her that

" All flesh is grass, and all the goodliness thereof is as the flower of the field.

The grass withereth, the flower fadeth ; but the word of our God shall stand forever."

INDEX

336

HAMILTON (Cont.)
 295 Alexander 69
 Mr 242
HANCOCK, L B 161
 188
HAND, Mr 316
HANNAFORD, Samuel
 316
HARKNESS, 301
 Anthony 252 299
 301 Emma 252
 Miss 253 Mr 253
 299 R P 317
HARMAR, Gen 8 23
 57 73
HARMON, Judge 227
 Judson 203
HARNISH, 263
HARRIS, 248 Andrew
 221 G W 317 J P
 189 John D 185
 Joseph 242 244
 295 Maj 255
HARRISON, Gen 26
 145 William Henry
 97 Wm H 127
HART, C P 229
HARTE, Francis Bret
 109
HARTWELL, G W 237
 John W 152

HARWOOD, Edward
 254 Mr 254
HAWLEY, Silas 212
HAYNES, Charles 148
HEALY, Caroline 188
HEFFNER, Mr 244
HEMANS, Mrs 217
HENRY, Joseph W
 319
HERBOLSHIMER, A
 188
HESS, Alfred 193
HIGHLAND, Dr 313
HILL, John W 188 236
 W H 98
HILLS, H B 322
 Henry A 188
 Howard B 321 Mr
 323 Mrs 323
 Townsend 322
HINSDALE, Loring
 172 224 Mrs Loring
 224
HOBSON, Gen 73
HOFFNER, Mr 135
 136
HOGE, Theudas 161
 188
HOLLIDAY, Thos 317
HOMBROOK, Richard
 189

338

KEITH, Robert 189
KELLOGG, Rev Mr
141
KELLY, S B 183
KELSALL, Wm W 198
KENNET, Col 140
John 140
KENNY, 92
KENZON, John 258
KERR, G W 188
KEY, Francis 290
Francis Scott 290
KEYES, R W 140
KEYS, Elders 286
Eleanor 246 Emma
252 Eva 265 John
F 265 273 285 286
Mr 252 253 273
285 Mrs 253 Mrs
John F 265 Mrs
Wm B 252 Richard
W 245 273 284
William B 246 Wm
B 252
KING, 264
KINMONT, Mrs M 304
KIRBY, 142 302 Clin-
ton 302 Mr 136
147 Mrs Clinton
302 T 136 Timothy
141

KNIGHT, Margaret
178
KNOWLTON, Ephraim
144 Mr 136 145
146
KOBERG, 258 259
KOEHLER, 184 Eliza-
beth 185
KRUG, Philip 188
LAFAYETTE, Gen 289
LANGLAND, Janet
142
LARUE, Geo S 236
LATTA, R B 314
LAWSON, Mrs Fenton
304
LEEPER, William 188
LEHRER, Mr 303
LEMON, Anna 301
LEUTHSTROM, Mrs
Wm 222 Wm 222
LEVOY, Michael 161
164 165 167 Mrs
Michael 167
LEVY, 298
LINCOLN, President
221 269
LOHMAN, Mr 158
LONGWORTH, Nicho-
las 127 311
LOVELL, Mrs Oliver

LOVELL (Cont.)
199 Mrs Oliver S
198 Oliver S 270
LOVETT, Mr 317
LOWE, J Harry 165
LOWELL, James
Russell 189
LOWEREE, E L 304
LOWES, James A 179
Mrs James A 179
LOWRY, Lt 33
LUDLOW, 133 279
Ben 133 Charlotte
Chambers 127 130
265 Dunlap 133
Israel 22 61 121
125 126 130 133
134 265 John 61
Mr 22 61 123
LUSE, A B 319
LUTHER, 260
LYONS, Albert 315
John G 314
LYTLE, Mrs Gen 265
William 127
M, Nettie 218
M'CAMMON, John
325
M'NAMARA, T E 181
MACE, John P 188

MADDUX, C B 237
MAHAN, 46 47 Mr 46
MAHER, Mr 303
MALEY, P F 317
MANSFIELD, 8 E D
126 Jared 8 126
MAPLESON, 281
MARPE, Capt 161 T H
188 Theodore 160
161
MARSH, Mr 255
Theodore 177
MARSTON, 100 J M
188
MARTIN, A 189 John
214
MATTHEWS, Judge
284 286 287
Mortimer 277 Mrs
Mortimer 277 Mrs
Stanley 140 274 S
295 Stanley 264
284 286
MAXWELL, 264
MAYHEW, Alexander
214
MCCAMMON, 318 323
John 326
MCCASHEN, James
41 42 John 42 44

WILKINSON (Cont.)
123
WILLIAMS, Hatfield
308 James R 179
180 Mrs James R
180 Samuel W 316
WILLIS, Elizabeth 38
Harry 304
WILMUTH, G W 308
Jane 185 207 Jane
Evatt 206 Mrs 207
214 Thomas 206
207
WILSON, Frank 188
WILTSEE, Chas S 188
W P 181
WINANS, John 42
Lewis 31 35
WINCHELL, Geo D
116
WINGENT, Ziba 44 45
WINGINA, 3

WITHENBURY, C W
191 304
WOODRUFF, 114 234
C S Jr 237 Charles
S 233 Mr 217 233
WORKUM, Levi J 198
WORTH, Gen 293
WORTHINGTON, T
127
WOUVERMAN, 263
WRIGHT, B F 189
Crafts J 282 Dr 71
E P 141 Helen M
319 John F 148
Mrs Crafts J 282
Thos 319
YEATMAN, W M 317
ZANT, Van 237
ZEILER, Lewis A 193
ZERBE, James S 100
155

www.ingramcontent.com/pod-product-compliance
Lightning Source LLC
Chambersburg PA
CBHW070548270326
41926CB00013B/2237